KT-116-656

Table of Contents

Chapter 1:

Your Triathlon Success Starts Here

Welcome to Triathlon for Beginners

Triathlon is one of the fastest growing sports around the world. You are joining a community of amazing people, with incredible focus, supporting each other to achieve more, surprise themselves and hit major bucket list goals.

That feeling of crossing the finish line never gets boring, whether it is your first triathlon or your 100th. It will bring you new friends, a new level of fitness, a younger looking body, more energy and a whole lot of fun.

Whether you are a man or a woman, black or white, have two legs or one leg, people of all shapes and sizes are joining in and getting involved. It is never to late to start. People in their 70s and 80s are competing within their age groups and inspiring the younger athletes.

To say you ran a marathon used to get the respect from people in the office. Sadly these days, it does not so much. But saying you "raced a triathlon" now earns the new level of respect and admiration.

Barriers to Entry

Many people look in admiration at you when you say you do triathlon. Usually the next sentence that comes of their mouth is, "Oh, I would love to do that but I can't because...."

These are the most common excuses:

1) The fear of how much time it takes to prepare for one

For some people, preparing for just a 5km run seems to take up their whole week.

They could not possibly contemplate fitting in 3 sports.

If this is you, and you have been tempted by triathlon but know there is so much to get your head around, I have written this book so you can shortcut your journey to success in triathlon as quickly as possible.

As long as you have a plan, it really does not have to take that much more time. Most people of average fitness can complete a short triathlon with minimal extra training. Just by squeezing in 30 minutes training at lunch-time or skipping your usual TV show, you can make a lot happen in your life without disrupting too much.

You can be very competitive in shorter triathlons with just 5-8 hours a week training. For longer triathlons, allow 10-12 hours a week training. But there is no need to be thinking about 30 hours a week time requirement.

2) The expense of all the gear you have to get

Again this is an irrational, illogical fear in many cases.

Sure, you *can* spend unlimited amounts on all the best gear, easily running into the thousands of dollars. But equally, you can get by for your first few races on relatively little.

I remember for my first race - a sprint triathlon - I borrowed a wetsuit from a friend, I had an old beat up mountain bike and some old trainers. I used some old bike shorts I already had and a running vest. As it was a short event, I did not need any specific gels or sports drinks and got by with water.

It really does not matter what you use as long as you have fun and do not talk yourself out of it before you have even begun. Seriously, people will NOT be looking at you or judging you. Everyone is nervous and only concerned with themselves.

Sure, I did not break any world records, but for my first one it was an amazing feeling just to finish and it got me excited. If I had waited until I was totally prepared, I never would have started!

Of course, then I went out and bought a racing bike and a tri suit, but only when I knew I was ready to take it more seriously.

And by the way, even with my very basic gear in my first race, I did not feel out of place for a minute, as there were plenty of people in the same position as me trying it out for the first time with the gear they already had.

Most of the excuses for why you have not started are just that: excuses!

Most of them are irrational.

Don't let the voice in your head steal your dreams!

3) The skill level required to start

The biggest fear is swimming if you are a weak swimmer (or cannot swim). Yes, you will have to take some lessons and do some practice. It is not impossible. If you book 10 lessons and do some practice, you should be ready to swim 400 meters in a few months.

Or you could start with duathlon and just run and bike until your swimming is good enough. Or book into a race with a pool swim so you are in no danger if you fatigue.

The bike and run all have technical aspects to them, which, if addressed, can improve your performance, but usually they are not a barrier to entry to getting started.

Most fears are based on nothing! So if there is something holding you back from something you want to achieve, identify what the fear actually is. Most of the time it will be irrational fear, which you can completely ignore. If there is something you need to address, like learning how to swim, then do that. Eliminate the fear and get on with your goal.

Remember, the time will pass anyway. So where do you want to be in 2 years time?

How to Use This Book

If you are a beginner, I advise reading this book from cover to cover to get a general overview about everything you need to know and where you should focus initially.

If you have a few races under your belt already, I have tried to be specific in the chapter headings and descriptions so you can quickly flip to the sections you need to improve your training and racing immediately.

One of the biggest skills you will learn in your triathlon journey is time management.

- How to fit it all in and STILL maintain a normal life
- How to fit it all in and not go completely mad
- How to fit it all in without upsetting your family and friends

It CAN be done but you need to learn to *train smarter*, not longer.

This book aims to give you exactly what you need to do to maximize your training results in the shortest period of time.

Purpose Of Every Session

Traditionally, triathlon training was all about lots of volume, training every spare minute you had to get some more miles in.

To be honest, some people still train like that but it is generally not sustainable. These people, overcome with triathlon fervor, usually end up burnt out or injured.

At www.triathlon-hacks.com the team and I aim to bring you all the best strategies to fast track your progress and get awesome results with minimal time out of your life.

I will make this the focus of this book too. There is *never* any need to do junk miles.

In other words, every training session needs to have a defined purpose, not just another bike ride or run without a specific aim. If you know what you are trying to get out the session, you generally engage mind and body and get exponentially better results.

In a later chapter I will discuss more about how to switch on the incredible power of the mind.

Triathlon is currently one of the fastest growing sports. It is an amazing event offering new challenges, well-rounded fitness and a great feeling of accomplishment when you cross the finish line. In fact, it is an ideal sport for everyone - any age, any gender, any body shape as you can get involved at whatever your fitness or skill level.

There are distances to suit everyone and you can achieve all your goals, whether they are weight loss, fitness, gaining a new social circle, increasing self-esteem or simply just feeling great, looking good and having fun!

I have endeavored to provide you with all the "gems" I have collected over the years from my racing, coaching and training-specific knowledge. These are the little insights that will help you break through your plateau periods, set new records you had not felt were possible and save you embarrassment on race day.

Plus, I have awesome tips and advice about nutrition, triathlon-specific strength training and mental attitude that you need to know but no one ever tells you.

This book will fast-track your progress and get you the knowledge that experienced triathletes have taken years to find out but which those new to the sport find daunting, embarrassing or simply unthinkable until something goes horribly wrong.

There is no need to learn through bitter experience, wasted time and effort. Instead, be smart and learn from those who have been there and done that. Triathlon is a social and really enjoyable sport with enough challenge to keep you going for a lifetime and enough rewards to satisfy your effort and application. Whether you love the technical side of it and all the gadgets or you love the challenge of the endurance, training and race tactics, this sport is for you!

Who Is This Book For?

This book is designed for you if you:

- Are curious about your first triathlon but are too scared to book your first race
- Have booked your first event and need more structure to your training plan
- Are quite competitive in one of the sports and are thinking of triathlon to challenge yourself or make training more interesting
- Have completed a few races and want to bridge the knowledge gap quickly to go to the next level

Pull The Trigger

Sometimes, to the outsider, triathlon can seem quite daunting: Lots of hidden rules, lots of clothing required and lots of gear.

A beginner's mind often sounds something like this:

"Everyone else is faster than me."
"They all know what they are doing."
"It looks too complicated and hard to do."
"What if I look stupid?"

This is completely natural - we ALL have these thoughts from time to time.

Just practice NOT listening to this voice!

When these thoughts enter your head, recognize them for what they are: absolute rubbish, complete drivel that will get in the way of your dreams.

Sure, do as much preparation as you can: read this book, talk to other people in the sport, join a few training sessions at a club but then *pull the trigger* and enter an event.

The quickest way to learn is to DO.

The first lesson you will learn by DOING a race is that it is not that scary!

You will notice there are people from all walks of life.

You will notice most people are there for a laugh and a good time and are not sponsored athletes.

You will notice most people do not have super expensive bikes and gear.

You will notice how supportive the other athletes and supporters are.

Maybe you've googled 'triathlon training', seen a few YouTube videos or spoken to friends, causing you to become confused or daunted. At the beginning there seems so much to learn that you might feel that you need 2 years of preparation.

You will be pleased to know this is not the case.

Most people of average fitness can do a sprint triathlon with just 6-8 weeks of preparation.

If you wish to do longer events, a few months to prepare will serve you well.

This book will bring it all together and focus on what works *in the minimal amount of time*.

The main idea of your first few triathlons is to enjoy the event, which will happen so much more if you are prepared. *Triathlon For Beginners* will provide the answers to many questions you may be struggling with right now such as:

- How do I train?
- How do I fit it all in?
- Can I just use my normal bike?
- What happens on race day?
- Do I need a special diet?
- How much gear do I actually need?

You will also find a whole load of information, articles, and resources on www.triathlon-hacks.com so stay in touch for updates, latest information and cutting edge research to keep you on top of your game.

Your First Race

If you are considering your first race, you are at the start of a great new adventure. Certainly, it will lead to better fitness, new friends, greater self-confidence and improved health.

There are skills and knowledge you need to supercharge your improvement. So you do not need to master everything to enter your first race.

If you have not started yet, learn the basics, then enter your first race. Do not get paralyzed by thinking you need to know and master it all. You can add the other skills as you grow and develop as an athlete.

If you are an intermediate who already have the basics you can jump straight into these extra skills and you will notice rapid improvements. Incidentally, a lot of people have come across these concepts but they don't take action.

If you do not *use* the knowledge you have gained, then you don't really know it.

For example, many people talk about sports psychology and mental toughness and how important it is. But very few people practice it regularly. When applied 10 minutes a day consistently, skills like these will give you results beyond what you thought was possible.

To be great you must do what others do not do!

Most people "wing it" on race day, then wonder why it felt so tough, or why they forgot their gels or why they drank too much water and had stomach cramps in the run.

I will go through each of these strategies in detail so you can devise a plan that you can implement daily, weekly and monthly. When race day comes, there will be no surprises and everything will go smoothly.

You can absolutely complete a triathlon. There is no barrier to entry and you will find triathlon is a really great world full of supportive people eager to help newcomers.

You will discover in this book all the information you need:

Smart bike training for people with minimal time

Improving your climbing and descending skills on the bike

Running technique tips which will take minutes off your time

Race start tips for the open water swim

The best swimming drills that will make the swim effortless

Race etiquette for swim lane racing in a pool

How to smash minutes off your transition time (easy when you know how)

How to avoid common injuries

Brilliant triathlon strength training (most people do not understand the importance of this)

How to structure a training plan

And I have also included some information that is harder to find:

- What to wear
- What to expect on your first race
- What to eat the morning of the race
- Race rules and regulations
- Mental toughness
- Fuelling and hydration strategies

Myth Busting

1. **Triathlon takes over your life.**

   There is a myth that if you are a triathlete you have to train all the time. Nothing could be further from the truth. Yes, some people do train all the time, but these people usually burn out in a couple of years. The idea is to train smarter.

   Planned correctly, triathlon training for any distance can be planned into a normal life balancing work and family commitments. For most people, switching a couple of nights of TV for some training or getting up half hour earlier will be more than enough to compete at a decent level.

2. **I'm too old.**

   Many people start triathlon in their 50's and 60's. It is NOT too late. And it is a sport you can do into your old age. The oldest triathlete in the world over 90 years old and he did not start until he was in his 70's. He has now done 41 triathlons and is still going strong!

   So age is no excuse! People from all walks of life, all ages and all colors compete, so do not let your own preconceptions hold you back.

   Many triathletes find that their times improve year after year as they get fitter and learn more about the sport. They also gain race experience and improve their mental toughness and stamina. You are never too old or too young to start, so stop thinking about it and start doing.

   Regular exercise and fitness will also slow down the ageing process, lower your stress levels, strengthen your immune system and give you lots more energy.

   Building lean muscle tissue maintains a healthy level of youthful hormones and keeps you looking and feeling younger for longer.

   Why not do something right now? That's right, stop reading,

get up and do 10 press-ups, then keep reading. You will feel better already having taken action towards your goal. The most important thing about a goal is doing an action towards it straight away!

3. Triathletes are superhuman freaks.

Triathletes get a certain reputation due to the Ironman and ultra Ironman distances. However, the majority of triathletes participate in races, which take 1-2 hours.

This is achievable with some general fitness and a bit of training. Triathlon does not have to take over your life and it can certainly fit into a normal life with work and family commitments.

4. It will take me away from my family.

If your partner is into sport or fitness, it is great to do shared training sessions sometimes. If you have a family, you can get the kids involved. They could ride their bikes as you jog along next to them. Or when you take them to swim training, instead of sitting on the sidelines wasting an hour of your life, jump in the adult pool and do a swim set yourself.

If you do have kids, they will be proud of having a fit mum or dad who looks amazing amongst the other parents, young, fit and fresh faced, instead of one who can only talk about the soap operas on TV, the special offer on the chocolate biscuits and how tired they are all the time.

5. It is super intense.

Actually, it is much less intense than doing just one sport. Think for a minute how many people take part in marathons around the world. These races take on average 4-6 hours and certainly place a lot of pounding stress on the body. Most of these people do no upper body exercise; they just run. That is intense on the body.

How much more balanced is triathlon with the swimming and cycling elements thrown in to balance the body both with much less pounding on your joints?

Besides, it is so much more interesting!

Triathlon will train not only your body, but also give you a healthy, well-balanced frame. It will also train your mind and your character.

What is triathlon?

Triathlon is a multi-sport event, which involves swimming, cycling and running and the 4th discipline, transition (which is changing from swimming to cycling (T1) and cycling to running (T2)). The race is in that order and must contain these disciplines to be a triathlon.

A bit of history

The first triathlon was held in 1975 in Mission Bay San Diego by a bunch of friends training together who thought it would be fun. It consisted of 6 miles of running, 5 miles of cycling and 500 yards of swimming. There was no entry fee and 46 athletes took part. Cross-training was not a term that had been coined at that stage.

In 1978 in Hawaii, people were arguing about which discipline required the greatest endurance. At that time Hawaii hosted The Waikiki Rough Water Swim (2.4 miles), The Oahu Bike Race (112 miles) and The Honolulu Marathon (26.2 miles). Originally events in themselves, they were rolled into one to become the 'Hawaii Ironman Triathlon.'

15 athletes competed and just 12 of them finished.

By 1982 the Hawaii Ironman Triathlon attracted coverage on ABC sports and had 580 athletes competing for glory. Now 1800 lucky triathletes compete to earn a coveted spot at this major event.

There are also many official Ironman events around the globe and many, many unofficial ones. And thousands of other events consisting of other distances.

Distances

There are various distances involved in triathlon but the official ones are:

- Sprint distance: 750m swim, 20km bike, 5km run
- Olympic/standard distance: 1.5km swim, 40km bike, 10km run
- Half Ironman/middle distance: 1.9km swim, 90km bike and 21km run
- Ironman/full distance: 3.8km swim, 180km Bike, 42km run

You will find other distances locally but these are the main ones.

Where do I start?

Most of you will already have a fair idea of what distance you want to start on, what your existing fitness level is and you will also probably have some vague goals.

A sprint distance is one almost anyone of average fitness can complete in without too much training so this is a good starting place.

Some athletes stay with this distance and easily fit it in their schedule with just 5 or 6 hours training a week.

There is a recent trend for beginners to jump straight into Ironman distance. Most of these people get a very harsh reality check and end up not completing the distance and never doing triathlon again! The best thing to do is a few sprint distances, then some Olympic distance races. The following year do a few half Ironman's/middle distance. Then the following year, schedule a full Ironman.

Of course, the full distance Ironman does take more time to train and more commitment. However, it is still possible to fit it in around your family and work commitments.

By the way, a full Ironman is not the ultimate goal of every triathlete and many are more than happy doing sprint and

Olympic triathlons for many years.

Do not wait until you have all the gear, all the strategies and all the training plans set up. Simply grab your bike and go, grab your swimming goggles and go, grab your running shoes and go. All the details can be refined later.

> **Success is the result of many small efforts repeated day in, day out.**

A great way to stay focused is to book a race a few weeks or months out (depending on your fitness). Once you have this date booked in, work backwards from that date so you know exactly what you have to achieve each week to accomplish it.

A training journal is essential. Start to write down your sessions, what you do and when. Set a goal, and then write down a plan to get you to that goal and DO NOT stop until you reach it.

> **Part of triathlon training is training your character to do the work even when you do not feel like it.**

Accept the challenge, stick to your program rigidly, whether it is raining outside or you just "don't feel like it". The feeling of success and achievement when you cross the finish line will taste even sweeter.

One advantage of triathlon training is there is always something you can do. So, for example, if your legs are tired from a hard run yesterday plus it is raining outside, you can make today your swim session or hit the gym and do a core strength session.

Building a base fitness

Base training is very important, particularly if you are unfit. But some athletes are fit in one sport but not another. If this is you, you need to be careful.

Let me give you an example: you might be fit for cycling or

swimming but not running. You decide to do a triathlon as you are already fit. Your cardio vascular system is already highly trained so when you start running, you may feel you could run forever.

However, for swimmers and cyclists, their muscles, tendons and joints are not used to the weight bearing stresses of running or pounding the streets.

If you are new to running, you must teach your body to do these new movements. You are training neuromuscular pathways. You must allow your joints, bones and tendons to adapt to the new loads placed upon them.

Joints and tendons take longer to adapt than muscles. Your aerobic base develops quicker than your joints and tendons. This is why so many runners develop Achilles tendonitis or shin splints. Your cardiovascular systems feel fine so you keep increasing the distance or intensity but you must allow enough time for your joints, muscles and tendons to adapt or they will develop pain and injury.

Build slowly and allow your body to adapt. Injury is the curse of the triathlete and usually results from doing too much too soon and thinking you are invincible. Play it steady, stick to your training plan and be disciplined about increasing your distance. Listen to your body, especially aches and pains. If you need a day off occasionally, take it. Base training may take between 2-6 months, depending on your existing level of fitness.

If you are overweight, it is a good idea to start swimming and cycling first to shed some body fat before pounding the pavements. Paying attention to your nutrition is the fastest way of losing weight, so do this at the same time. There is a whole chapter dedicated to nutrition coming up later.

For the purposes of triathlon, every extra pound you carry slows down your run by 2 seconds per mile and on a bike by 3 watts of power. This means you will add 10% to your race times at least!

Try to maintain and raise your resting metabolic rate. You do this by eating regular small meals throughout the day. Do not skip meals, especially breakfast. Add muscle tone to your body by strength training. More active muscle tissue raises your resting metabolic rate so you will burn more calories, even at rest. Stop eating just before you are full and reach for whole, natural foods rather than manufactured, highly-processed foods.

Basic training rules

Rule 1: **Never increase distance or duration by more than 10% a week.** If you do, you will run the risk of getting injured.

Rule 2: You improve when you rest. Always schedule rest into your training plan. This includes a rest day at least once a week. It also includes an easy week training every 4-6 weeks where you drop the intensity and duration down and allow your body to recover.

You will be able to come back to training harder the following week, mentally fresher and more focused.

Rule 3: Keep a training journal. This is an important habit to get into. Many triathletes think that they should train based on how they feel that day.

Training based on "how you feel" will not lead to great success on a consistent basis.

You must plan your sessions in advance, then execute the session according to your plan.

Write down every session you do. Include the distance, discipline, sets, how you felt, times and any other details you recorded like heart rate, average speed or power. It will give you a sense of accomplishment when you look back and see how much you have progressed. It can also help identify weaknesses or areas of improvement. Also, make sure you record when you eat, what you ate beforehand, during and after. You are looking for patterns and testing out what your body responds to best.

There are many ways to keep a training journal, including pencil and paper. Experiment for a while with which method and format works best for you.

If you take on a coach at some point, it will be far more effective if you can discuss your actual training and your results over the previous 2 years, not just a general overview of whatever you remember.

> **Once you start keeping a journal you will be amazed at how bad your memory really is.**

Sometimes you may feel like you had a bad month training but when you look back at your journal, you see that you achieved all your goals for the month and made huge progress. Maybe you just happened to feel tired in the last few days, which clouded your memory of the whole month.

With our very pressurized time limitations of work, family, training and social activities, a training journal will help you maximize each session and only do highly effective training rather than just junk miles. Junk miles are a waste of time, add nothing to your strength or fitness and simply increase your likelihood of being injured.

A training journal will also allow you to track when you train best, and see if you are favoring one discipline over the others. It will help you see where your weaknesses are and it will help you structure your next month's training more effectively.

What To Add To Your Training Journal

- the type of training you did
- average heart rate
- power output
- distance
- steady state versus interval training
- what time of day

- the weather conditions
- how well you slept
- fatigue
- muscle soreness or any aches and pains
- how you felt beforehand
- how you felt afterwards
- what you ate before, during and after training

Keep going to get as much information as you can. This should not be a chore and should only take a few minutes. You can write it in a journal or log it on a computer.

You should also identify at the beginning of the journal what your goals are for the year, and when you want to achieve them.

This will be a massive help when you are planning your training. You will be clear about how fit and strong you need to be at certain times of the year, you can schedule in time to taper before an event, and you can schedule in recovery after hard sessions or races.

Be clear about what you want to achieve, then break this down into six month, three month and monthly goals. This will help structure your training plan.

What Is Your Why?

You should identify why you are doing this. This will help you stay motivated when it is raining outside and you simply want to stay inside under the duvet (this happens more frequently than you might think). You need to remember your "why" and get up and train anyway.

The reasons might include:

- My friends are doing it
- To lose weight
- To complete a new challenge

- To remain fit and healthy
- To beat my 17-year-old son

Whatever the reasons are, write them down on page one of your journal so that when it is raining and you do not want to go cycling or running, simply read your "why", then put your shoes on and go.

You know you will feel great afterwards.

An accurate training journal is one of the most powerful training tools you have as it will allow you to look back, see what has worked, what hasn't worked, what your body responds to best and areas you can improve.

Also, you get a massive motivational boost from just seeing how much you have improved over the year. It will make all the hard training worth it. You will not believe how much your body can change and adapt in such a short space of time.

A training journal will also warn you about possible injury or sickness, because often you will notice warning signs in advance. For example, if a cold or flu is developing you may notice a higher heart rate for less effort a week before you develop symptoms. This is a sign to take it a bit easier. You may notice a tight feeling in your calf when running several days or weeks in a row. You may need to get a sports massage or increase your stretches to prevent an imminent calf tear.

Most importantly, keep it simple. If keeping a training journal becomes a chore, you will give up and not do it at all. Your journal really should only take you a few minutes after a session.

As with most things in triathlon, discipline and consistency is everything.

There are some online programs available but if you do your own excel spreadsheet or use a pen and paper, it is free, easy and so very powerful. If you have not started doing this, start today!

Rapid Recovery

On the issue of rest, one of the most underestimated parts of training is recovery.

In fact, rest is so important I have put it at the beginning instead of bolting it on at the end as an afterthought.

Recovery, you say? Surely, this is the easy part. I lie down, chill out and the next time I get up, I will be fine. What could there possibly be to know about recovery?

You will be surprised how addictive triathlon can be.

You will also be surprised to learn many triathletes on their "rest" day do a sneaky training session in the hope they will improve faster!

Rapid recovery is the key to getting yourself back in a state of readiness for training the next day as well as fulfilling all your other commitments like doing your work, attending to your family and getting on with life in general.

It is also the key to avoiding being so sore and tired for days that you become a misery to yourself and those around you.

Here are the top 9 secrets that will guarantee you a fast recovery:

1. Sleep

The importance of good sleep cannot be overstated. It is during our sleep that our growth hormone starts to work repairing muscles, damaged bones, joints, blood cells and fuel systems to make us adapt and be stronger, fitter and ready for more.

This is so important that the latest research (Stanford Sleep Disorders Clinic and Research Laboratory) has found that extra sleep resulted in an uncharacteristic number of personal best times for a group of athletes they tested.

Make sure you get 7-9 hours sleep each night.

Try to sneak in a 20-30 minute nap in the afternoon.

Try not to train or eat late at night, both of which make it hard to go to sleep.

2. Quality nutrition

Nutrition provides the building blocks to all your cells, fuel to your muscles and aids all the metabolic processes in your body. If you eat garbage, you will get garbage results.

Very simple.

Choose natural whole foods as much as possible like fresh fruit, vegetables, grains, and fresh organic meats. Avoid excess sugar, fat and processed junk.

Eating the right food during training will enhance your recovery. Make sure you are getting plenty of protein to help muscle repair. Other important nutrients include iron to support the blood and zinc to assist healing.

Both of these are found in meat and whole grains.

Add plenty of water, not sugary sports drinks to your diet.

A poor diet cannot be compensated for on race day by magic gels and supplements.

Eat right all the way along. It will assist your training, your recovery and your results!

3. Cross-training

Low impact workouts like elliptical training, rowing machine training or rollerblading are brilliant for keeping your fitness up without pounding your muscles.

It also gives you a mental break from the track, bike and pool, which can make you feel a lot better. Cross-training keeps the blood flowing through the muscles and changes the movement patterns so it keeps you fresh and your muscles alert.

4. Cooling down and stretching

Cooling down and stretching can assist recovery greatly as it keeps blood flowing through the muscles, gradually reduces the heart rate and allows lactic acid and waste products to flush out instead of collecting in the muscles, making them ache the next day.

Stretching lengthens out tight muscles that have been working hard and prevents the buildup of tight knots, which can predispose an athlete to injury.

It is also crucial for preventing muscle imbalance. This is where we do the same repetitive activities day in, day out, and some muscles tend to get tighter and tighter (for example, hip flexors, hamstrings and calves). Stretching will help prevent knots or tears in these muscles.

5. Sports massage

Massage breaks down areas of tight knots and scar tissue developed from hard workouts and helps maintain muscle length. It also helps with the resolution of lactic acid and other waste products and helps maintain muscle length.

No matter how great you are at stretching, not all the fibers in your muscles will get stretched out properly again. Over time problem areas and knots can develop in muscles. Massage will identify this quickly and address it right away.

See a sports physiotherapist or sports massage therapist (not a beauty therapist) who is used to dealing with athletes and their injuries for massage.

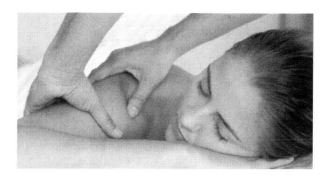

6. Self massage

You can try to do self-massage with your hands, or buy a <u>foam roller</u> to roll on.

A <u>foam roller</u> is a great tool for keeping most problems at bay and maintains the extendibility in your muscles. It works well for ilio tibial band (the side of the thigh notorious for causing problems in runners), quadriceps, hamstrings and calves. Warning: it can be very painful. Go easy for the first few times; it will get easier!

Roll on the problem area for 1-2 minutes until the pain dissipates.

This is okay for maintenance but if you do have long term aching muscles or any injuries please just see an expert. Much better, quicker and more effective! Let them sort it out and get your focus back on your training, not your injury!

7. Hydration

Hydration is one of the most under-estimated tools you have to ensure your performance is peak. Just losing 2% of water results in a 30% decrease in performance (Armstrong et al, 1985).

Water has many functions. It helps eliminate metabolic waste products (like lactic acid) quickly, helps you control your body temperature through sweat, lubricates joints and helps digest food.

Always have a bottle of water with you in the office, at home and while you are training. The average sedentary person needs 6-8 glasses a day. As an athlete you need at least 12-16 glasses a day. Remember, some of this will come from food like fruit and vegetables. Do not wait until you feel thirsty before drinking. By then it is too late.

If you are doing a long session make sure your drink includes some sodium and electrolytes as you lose these in sweat.

8. Avoiding germs after hard sessions and races

When you are training very hard or recovering after a race, your immune system is at its lowest. Athletes are well known for often picking up colds or flu.

Try to avoid very hard sessions prior to jumping on a plane or air conditioned coach. Make sure you wash your hands before eating and keep your immune system boosted all the time by taking multi vitamins.

Athletes often underestimate the sleep they require. If you are run-down, training hard and trying to fit it all in, you will require extra sleep.

9. Correct planning of training sessions and races

As you increase the intensity of your sessions you will need to adjust the volume.

Have a look at your training sessions and make sure you build in some rest time. After a 6-8 week block of gradual building up, include some recovery time after each race and keep yourself fresh.

Preparation phase: Generally this takes between 3 and 6 weeks and gets your body used to training. It is a good place to commence drills and technique.

Base phase: This can last anywhere between 12 and 24 weeks. This phase focuses on building your aerobic capacity, technique and skills. There are usually different phases within this (for example, 3-4 week blocks followed by a rest then an increase in duration). Base training is the first focus of any training plan, then endurance, then speed and finally power.

Build phase: This phase drops the volume but increases the intensity. It aims to get you faster at a certain distance or to go further in a certain time. It will contain a lot of interval work and usually lasts around 4-8 weeks. As you proceed through your training I will ask you to shift to different heart rate zones and shift from largely aerobic training to anaerobic.

Taper phase: A week or two before a race you will need to cut back the volume and intensity to allow your body to recover and come to a race in peak condition. Use the time you would have been training to focus on your flexibility, mental attitude and race visualization. You are still training but much less, focusing on technique instead.

I will teach you how to structure the best workouts to get the most out of them. You will be training harder and smarter. The one thing you need to ditch is junk miles. These are miles just for the sake of it, which achieve absolutely nothing except potential injury. Before you commence each session you will know what the outcome is and how it will get you closer to your triathlon goal.

As a general rule you will need to do 20-25% swimming, 40-50% cycling and 20-25% running. Of course, if you have a particular weakness, do spend time practicing that one and, if necessary, get coaching in it.

Breaking your training into phases like this helps you understand what you are meant to be doing and why. It helps keep you disciplined with short-term targets and stops you from getting burnt out. You can't train at high intensity all the time. I will go into more detail about these phases and give you a sample training plan towards the end of this book.

Potential Obstacles

As with any plan, when you make it, obstacles suddenly appear.

So, let's tackle them now.

Time

This is the biggest hurdle for all of us. You, like many people, may have a busy career, family commitments, friends and a successful sporting life.

Really examine your day. A 24-hour day consists of 3 x 8 hours.

Let's say 8 hours is for sleep, 8 hours is for work. There is still enough time to do a few household chores, spend time with the family and fit in some training.

Look at areas of your day that are wasted. See if you could arrange things differently. Be really strict with yourself. Is there wasted time in front of the TV or trawling the internet for stuff you do not really need? Could you do all the shopping once a week instead of going to the shops every day?

Start to practice scheduling yourself first instead of last.

Write down the times you will train each week and fit the rest of your week around that.

It is amazing how much you can fit in if you have to. Most tasks expand to fit the time we give them. Do not let DIY, the house or gardening get in your schedule before your training.

Know How

This book will hold you by the hand to show you what you need to know. I have been there, done that, made every mistake. This book will help you short cut the typical mistakes beginner triathletes make in order to maximize your time and enjoyment.

Triathlon involves skill as well as fitness. Most beginners just focus on fitness.

This is a mistake as you then usually later have to unlearn most of your bad habits and relearn proper technique. If you can - at the beginning WHILE you are improving your fitness – remember to learn correct form and good technique. Practice this along the way as your fitness develops.

I will discuss good technique and some drills for swim, bike and run as we go through each section. Look out for this and implement this now - do not wait to do this in 2-3 years time.

Another important point to highlight now is that most athletes have a weakness.

Some of us know what our weaknesses are. For example, "I can't swim" is a common one. Make sure you spend time practicing your weaknesses. If you need some coaching, book 10 lessons. This is often much cheaper than you think.

Many people ignore their weakness hoping to "just get round" on race day.

This is foolish. Ignore the temptation to spend most of your training time practicing your strengths (because you enjoy them) and be disciplined enough to get stuck into turning an historic weakness into a new strength.

I will discuss nutrition, swim, bike and run techniques, equipment, bike maintenance, training plans, strength training, core stability and so much more, you will feel like an expert by the end.

Most people do not take the time to prepare much at all. In fact, by reading this book you will know more than most people who have done triathlon for two or three years.

Your mind

There will be many obstacles along the way; the biggest one is your own mind!

Fear and self-doubt, the little voice inside your head asking:

"What am I doing here? All these other people look so much better than me!"

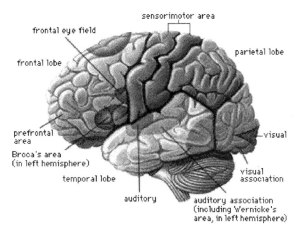

"The water looks rough. Maybe I should just go home now!"

"How many hills are there? Oh no, I will never make it!"

Guess what, you are not alone. Everyone faces these questions, nerves and self-doubt from time to time. Part of training is preparing your body for the challenges that lie ahead, but what many people do not realize is that part of the training is mental and preparing your mind for the challenge of training and racing is critical.

Triathlon provides so much variety, anyone of any level of fitness can compete. You can fit it into your busy schedule around work, kids and family commitments and it is a supportive and inclusive environment.

There are fantastic, well-respected role models like Chris McCormack, the Brownlee brothers and Dave Scott who have shown it can be done and give us all huge amounts of focus and inspiration. They have high profile careers in their own right with decent sponsorship and prize money. So, let's get you started.

Who knows where you could be a year from now?

Train smart!

I will break each of the disciplines down for you into their components.

This is the nuts and bolts of triathlon. I have included some technical tips, some race knowledge and important things we have learnt along the way that you can't get from typical triathlon books. So here goes: enjoy the book, absorb it in small chunks, do not allow yourself to be overwhelmed and join me on your incredible journey to triathlon success!

Chapter 2:

Advice to Triathletes Who Hate Swimming

Have you ever noticed that when a fish swims, it hardly seems to move?

It is not madly flapping its fins 30 times per minute. There is a small movement followed by a long glide. There are occasional small movements to change direction. Of course we are very different anatomically to a fish. However, similar principles apply.

When you observe a poor swimmer in a pool there is a lot of flapping and splash and awkward body movements side to side and up and down. There is very little or no glide at all.

It looks more akin to a washing machine turned on full power: a lot of spinning but going nowhere fast!

However, when you observe a great swimmer like an Olympian there is very little splash, there is a lot of gliding; they use long, slow deliberate strokes. It looks effortless.

Model how these great swimmers move.

Many triathletes cannot swim a stroke at the beginning of their training. Do not let this stop you.

I suggest booking some lessons and scheduling some regular time to practice.

You can get an idea of how to swim from books, DVDs and internet resources but swimming is so technical that it is likely you will pick up bad habits that you are unaware of. Use these resources as back up for your face-to-face lessons.

One to one feedback is the fastest way to improve at swimming.

Swimming well is ALL about technique, and time spent learning this at the beginning will save you so much anguish later. In triathlon conserving energy at the beginning is critical, as you still have to complete two more sports after the swim.

Unfortunately, many triathletes finish the swim completely exhausted and struggle to finish the bike and run. Aim to make the swim effortless. When you are training, aim for efficiency.

Once you have had some lessons, regular practice is essential.

Joining a master's swim squad or a tri club will help you concentrate on triathlon specific drills and swim sets. Joining a squad will also help you train properly and with varied intensity instead of aimlessly going up and down the pool at a relaxed pace.

Even if you are a good swimmer, a couple of "style correction" coaching sessions per year is really valuable to keep improving.

Olympic swimmers still have coaches and video many training sessions and races to observe their form and see where they can improve. Never be too arrogant to take advice.

Open water starts

Most triathlons are held around lakes or the sea. Few are in pools so open water swimming is the discipline triathletes need to develop and get used to.

Open water swimming terrifies many hard-core triathletes and is one of the biggest obstacles for beginners thinking about their first triathlon.

Open water is a world away from the comfort zone of a nice warm swimming pool doing a few laps following a black line up and down.

The athlete must cope with the demands of currents, waves, temperature and seaweed, not to mention other competitors.

Also, there is the prospect of a "pack start" where hundreds or thousands of triathletes start a race together. It can be very daunting if swimming is not your strongest discipline and you can get a lot of splashing and kicking around you.

Having said that, it is a skill you can learn and practice and who knows? One day maybe even get to like!

Tips for Easy Open Water Swimming

Sighting

One of the major skills you must learn is called "sighting". This is where you lift your head out of the water every four or five strokes just before you breathe and see where you are heading. Look out for the buoys as markers.

However, if the water is choppy seeing the buoys will be impossible. So make sure before you start the race to pick out some fixed landmarks on the land to guide you. If you go off course for a few hundred meters it can quickly drain your energy and your morale!

For example, you may see a building you will aim for on the way out as you head west along the bay, then a boat out at sea. Then, when you turn around, you might aim for the clock tower back on the shore.

The worst thing you can do is follow another swimmer, thinking that they know where they are going, because if you are having trouble then they could well be having the same problems and have less of an idea how to solve them than you do. Make your own plan and stick to it.

After you have improved your basic swimming technique, sighting is something you will need to practice in training. Add it to your drills once a week.

Swim 500m, alternating between 25m normal swimming and 25m "sighting". Every 4-5 strokes lift your head; try to keep moving forward as you do this without disrupting your flow. Make sure you don't actually stop to look up; this will be exhausting. Focus on staying as horizontal as you can, keep kicking, lift up, take a quick look and then get your head straight down again and get back to your normal breathing rhythm.

Very different muscles are required to sight. If you do not practice this you will become fatigued very quickly.

This is a great tactic for getting ahead of your competition as most people will not practice this. You will find many will fade away towards the end of the swim, while you will still feel strong.

Position in the pack

When there is a bunch of swimmers, it is not uncommon to get kicked, which can really spoil your race, especially if you get kicked in the face. If you are a strong swimmer, swim hard at the beginning and get away from the pack. If you are not a strong swimmer then let the better swimmers go ahead so you can focus on your race with less bother from them trying to swim over you.

Some people have the strategy of starting on the edge of the pack so they are not bunched up in the middle and this can also work.

Know the course in advance

Doing some homework about the course and the conditions is always a good idea. Try to do a few swims in similar conditions. If it is a lake swim, find some local lakes and swim the same race distance. Always be safe and swim with buddies and make sure there is someone on land watching you with a cell phone and/or safety devices.

Likewise, if it is an ocean swim, practice some ocean swims. Get used to the currents and temperatures and learn to relax in the ocean.

Do not make race day your first ocean swim!

There is enough going on and enough pre-race nerves without adding the stress of a new environment to the mix. If you have the opportunity to check out the exact stretch of ocean or lake before the race, this is a great idea. Chat with the locals or the lifeguards about the current and tides. Plan your strategy.

Check if the current is strong and which way it is going. If it is running to the right make sure that you start the race on the left end of the start line, then swim with your sight on the left side of the buoy. You will be pulled to the right by the current and have to fight it much less than if you start at other end of the start line.

Another strategy is to start at the side that you breathe on. If you breathe to the right then start with the pack on your right so you can see them.

Of course if you have learned bilateral breathing, this will not be a problem.

Races are generally pretty safe these days, and there are precautions to stop any serious injuries in the sea. However, incidents still sometimes occur, so take open water swimming seriously and ensure you get as strong as possible.

The 9 Secrets to Amazing Swim Technique

Start swimming training early in the season. Swimming requires practice, practice and more practice. Do not leave it thinking you can "catch up" later. Start early and be consistent. No matter how hard you train, if you have poor technique, swimming will always be a struggle.

Just because you are fit for running and cycling does not mean you are fit for swimming. Many athletes who are super fit in another sport are shocked at how breathless they get just swimming 25 meters. Also, on race day anxiety, nerves and cold water can sometimes make breathing very difficult. You will be a whole lot more in control and ready for the bike if you are confident and strong in your swimming.

1) Frequency

Frequency is important. Frequent shorter sessions will help you become a better swimmer faster than a long session once or twice a week.

This will help you develop a "feel" for the water. This will give you that sense of power and control in the water, the sense that every stroke counts and gives you significant forward propulsion.

2) Relaxation

The key to powerful swimming is relaxation. Allow yourself to play in the water a bit. Let yourself sink down, and then come back up for air, Sink down again, relax.

Next, push off the wall, on the surface this time, and just stretch out and kick. Push off the wall and see how far you can go under water. Hold onto the edge and practice breathing out while your face is in the water (blowing bubbles), turning your head and inhaling air.

Power and speed in swimming come through relaxation and being streamlined.

How often do you see swimmers training where a huge, muscular, fit-looking man is being out-lapped easily by a skinny, 14-year-old girl?

Answer: all the time!

You do not need to pack on upper body muscle to swim fast.

Focus on technique and the speed will come.

Drill:

Try swimming a few laps with very relaxed arms. Over exaggerate the relaxation. Make sure your arms are not stiff or clenched. Practice soft entry into to water with minimal splash. During the pull through, remain relaxed. Focus on feeling the water as you pull through.

3) Reduce Drag

A major rule in swimming is reducing drag. Your head can cause a lot of drag. Aim to be as streamlined as possible. Don't look forward. Instead, always imagine you are swimming downhill and look down at the bottom of the pool. Imagine leading with the top of your head, not your forehead.

Tennis Ball Drill

Practice swimming with your head in the proper downward position by finding a tennis ball-sized inflatable ball and placing it between your chin and neck. Practice swimming and breathing while still holding this ball between your chin and neck.

Imagine your core is a rigid pole while you are swimming. Rotate your body on the imaginary pole. This is one reason why swimmers do not need big arm muscles. Technique, position in the water and a strong core helps propel them forward and does not dissipate energy.

Kicking technique is important too. This will give you forward momentum and also help you maintain your body position, especially in open water racing. Do not ignore kicking sets. Buy yourself a kick board and get busy doing kick drills.

4) Good body position

Good body position is essential to good swimming. A lot of swimmers find swimming exhausting as their legs drop and drag along. This is like swimming with a lead weight attached to your ankles.

The hips should be high in the water and the feet up, kicking near the surface. The problem occurs where swimmers lift their head to breath and swim with their head high. When the head is high, the legs will sink.

The best way to achieve this position is to stretch out in the water and put your head down.

Most new swimmers swim with their head too high. The head should be down with the water level running right across the top, at the crown of the head. Keep your head down while holding it in line with your spine and shoulders. This way your entire front half will also go down in a nice line and your hips will come up. Look down at the bottom of the pool, not forward.

If your head is raised, your feet and legs will drop, and it will feel like a dead weight is being dragged behind you. Keep your head down and your legs will pop up.

Relax. If your body is too rigid while doing any of this, it will cause excess fatigue and prevent you from developing a smooth, long stroke.

5) Develop Powerful Arms

This does not mean to hit the weights room! This means good technique. ☺

Think about swimming tall. You need to think about your body slipping through the water with the least resistance possible. When your arm enters the water, think about it entering through a tiny hole with no splash.

Swim like a springboard diver with minimum splash.

Aim for long, relaxed strokes. Many swimmers have short, inefficient strokes. When you reach out in front, try to extend your arm an extra inch and rotate your body a bit to help get more length.

Enter the water in front of your shoulder, not across the midline.

Bring your arm back under you with a bent elbow. This is a much stronger position than swimming with a straight arm. Think about pulling through with all your forearm and hand, not just your hand. Make as large a surface area as possible.

Also, think about pulling your body forward over your hand rather than pulling your hand back towards you.

Closed Fist Drill

This is a tough one but it really gives you a sense of "feel" of the forearm contributing to the forward momentum. It will feel extremely difficult and pointless at first (like most drills) but persist with it as it really helps.

Try swimming with a closed fist so you can't use your hands. Think about using your forearm to propel you forward. Swim 50 meters with your fists closed, then 50 meters with open hands, still focusing on getting propulsion from your forearms. The difference in forward propulsion is amazing.

Recovery Stroke

On the recovery part of the stroke, think about bringing your hand through with a high elbow. Do not do a roundhouse action. This is inefficient and wastes time. Again, focus on relaxed hands and arms.

Zipper Drill:

A great drill for this is to run your fingers up your side as you bring your arm through like you are doing up a zipper.

As you rotate to breathe, rotate on your axis; do not flail about all over the place.

6) Breathing

Breathing is one of the most asked-about subjects when it comes to swimming.

It is the area most people, even very good athletes, struggle with.

The biggest mistake beginners make is not exhaling fully when their face is in the water.

The key is to blow ALL the air out, and then breathe in when your head turns. It should be rhythmic and controlled.

Where some people go wrong is they only blow half the air out (or hold their breath) then they have to lift their head, quickly blow out, then breathe in and then put their head down again.

This makes their legs start to sink because their head is up and they spend the rest of the swim fighting the water instead of gliding through it. This uses excessive energy and they are forced to breathe harder to gasp for air and the whole problem becomes worse!

Breathing Drill

Remember, breathe in all the way and breathe out all the way.

This is so important that you need to practice it on its own without thinking about your arms and legs and staying buoyant at the same time. So grab a kickboard and swim, holding it out in front with both hands. Stroke and breathe normally: breathe in relaxed, then put your face in the after and exhale fully, then turn your head to the side and take a relaxed breath in. Do your swim strokes as normal.

The other way you can practice is to hold onto the side of the pool and do the same thing: do a stroke, turn your head and breathe in, do another stroke, and breathe out. Repeat focusing on the rhythm of breathing in and out easily and relaxed.

Do not gasp for breath; there is enough time if you stay calm and relaxed. Practice this. It will pay huge dividends.

The worst thing you can do is to take huge gulps of air, then hold your breath for too long. You will become really fatigued.

7) Gliding

Gliding is the KEY to swimming well. This is the major secret that professionals take years to master. Start thinking about it now. The aim is to use the minimum number of strokes to get to the other end. Use the streamlined glide for your momentum. Remember, strong stroke, then glide.

Gliding Drill

When training in a pool, count the number of strokes it takes you to get to the other end.

Over the next few weeks try to reduce this number. Michael Phelps (gold medalist Olympic swimmer) takes 7 strokes to get to the end of a 25m pool. Most swimmers who are reasonably well trained take 13-15 strokes and most beginners take about 20-25 strokes.

When you count your strokes make sure you do a glide in between each stroke. Slow your strokes down. Start with your arms out in front of you. Do one stroke, bring your fingertips back together, then glide. The do the same with the other arm. Repeat.

It is quite a difficult exercise. If it is too difficult at the beginning,

start by holding on to a kickboard to give you some buoyancy.

8) Kicking

Kicking is important. Try to think about your feet as fins helping to propel you forward. Keep your feet relaxed but your legs strong and taut. Do not kick from your knees. This is inefficient and fatigues your quadriceps - not a good idea when you have a cycle and run coming up.

Instead, kick from your hips with a strong, stable core.

Think about small powerful kicks, not big flailing kicks that disrupt the streamline of your body.

9) Get Video

If you have swum for a few years, even if you are quite advanced, video is an amazing way to improve. It provides incredible feedback that is meaningful to you.

When I am in a big swim squad and the coach is pointing out a drill or technique, sometimes I don't know if it applies to me or not.

When you look at a video of yourself you will clearly see whether you are lifting your head or crossing the midline with your hand entry.

One club I joined rented an above water camera and under water camera once a month to video everyone. It was amazing to see. The camera does not lie!

But even if you cannot get access to this, get a friend to take a simple video on your smart phone of you swimming. It is so valuable. Watch it later and compare it to YouTube videos of Olympic swimmers. It will be even better if you can show a swim coach who might point out things you are unaware of.

Pool Swim Race Etiquette

Some races conduct the swim in a local pool. This comes with its own challenges.

With several people to a lane on race day, how do you possibly overtake without running into swimmers coming the other way and inducing "lane rage"?

The main area of opportunity to overtake is at the wall when you touch to turn round. If you are competent, you can come in fast, do a tumble turn and push off hard. You will be well on your way before the swimmer in front even knew you were there. If tumble turning is not your thing, you will need to come in fast, touch and push off hard with a quick few strokes to get away and not hold them up.

Whatever happens, do not swim over anyone. Going around people mid lane only works if there are only two of you to a lane. If there are three or more, wait for the wall.

Proper pool etiquette is to touch the swimmer in front of you on the foot to let them know you are there; they should let you go at the next turning. The same goes for you. If you feel someone touching your feet, wait at the wall and let them go ahead.

When you are at the race, the marshal in the race briefing will tell you how many laps you must swim. However, it is wise to have worked this out beforehand and practiced the exact length several times. Use the briefing for confirmation, not new information!

So count your laps as you go. It is your responsibility. Often the marshal will have a system for confirming the number of lengths you have swum and will either shout at you when you have two laps to go or tap you on the head.

Make sure you know what they will do so you do not get a shock. ☺

The Gear

Wetsuit

Buy your own gear if possible! Test it, train in it and get to know it.

It is possible to hire a wetsuit if it is your first race and you don't know if you will carry on. But once you know that you will do triathlon for a season or two it is much better to buy your own wetsuit.

One of the most challenging parts of triathlon can be getting the wetsuit off when it is wet!

I know of cases where the athlete had to get cut out of their wetsuit in transition. No joke! Some athletes apply Vaseline around the neck, ankles and wrists to ease this. This can save you valuable minutes.

Either way, practice this several times until you can confidently get out of it in less than 20 seconds. The pros do it in 3-4 seconds. Many beginners take over 10 minutes!

I remember in my first triathlon I was exhausted coming out of the water. I was dizzy and disorientated. I could not remember where my bike was. There was a lot of shouting - marshals shouting instructions, supporters shouting encouragement. It was all a blur.

Finally I found my bike and started to remove the wetsuit. I can't remember the actual time but it felt like forever and was a real struggle! In the end I was so dizzy I had to sit on the ground to remove the wetsuit from my ankles as they just would not budge.

Needless to say, by the time I got on the bike, I was just about ready to lie down in a dark room!

The correct way

Unzip the top of the wetsuit as you leave the water and are running to the bike. Once at the bike, take the wetsuit off right down to the ankles in one go (1 second). Then stand on one wetsuit leg and kick one ankle out (1 second).

Repeat on the other side (1 second).

Help you go faster

As well as keeping you warm, wetsuits are also great because they aid buoyancy and make you swim faster. However, in a sprint distance, you need to weigh up whether the time it takes you to get the thing off is worth the time it saves you!

Check with the race organizers about the compulsory use of wetsuits as there are regulations around this. If the temperature of the water is below a certain level they will make you wear one or you will not be allowed to race.

Goggles

Goggles come in various shapes and sizes. If possible, get a range and test them out.

It is a good idea to have two pairs - one tinted for sunny days and one without tint for cloudy days. It is also a good idea to bring two pairs of goggles on race day in case a strap snaps or you lose a pair. Make sure they are both anti fog so you can see the buoys in an open water race easily.

Make sure that they are comfortable and that they don't leak. Whilst it is easy in a pool to stand up and remove water from your goggles, it is impossible in open water when you can't stand up.

If you are wearing a race-timing chip, make sure it is tightly secured on a band underneath your suit and on your ankle.

Race Day

Remember your form and your drills!

Incredibly, in the stress of the race and the panic of the start gun, many athletes who know how to swim properly go straight back to flailing about, using short, inefficient strokes, lifting their head and gasping for air.

The swimmers who lose their technique will fatigue in 1-2 minutes and come out of the water completely exhausted. Those who come out of the water first are those who remember their technique and get there with minimum strokes, minimum fuss, and a streamlined body.

Remember, relax your breathing, relax your stroke, glide, focus on your technique and do not panic.

Chapter 3:

Bike Brilliance

What Bike?

The bike is a subject that triathletes can talk about for hours and hours.

If you are at the beginning of your triathlon journey do not get distracted by which bike to get and how much to spend. Just get started!

If you have a bike that works, just get going. If you can borrow a family or friend's bike, do that. If you don't have a bike but you can get to spin class or find an exercise bike use that!

The most important thing is to get started.

Although you will see some very expensive looking bikes at every triathlon, the most important thing is the fitness and strength of the rider. A good bike will certainly enhance a good rider but the best bike used by an untrained, unfit, over weight person does not go any faster.

At many sprint events, all manner of bikes appear – from the dusty old bike out of Grandma's garage to the latest several-thousand-dollar carbon-fiber creation.

Obviously, the more you spend, the better your ride will be and the better you will perform - to some extent. But you do not need a very expensive bike to do a triathlon, so do not let that be a reason to put it off for another year. Borrow one, hire one or buy a cheap bike and compete.

When the time is right, obviously a bit of investment here will make your training and racing that much more enjoyable.

What sort of price range is decent?

For $750 - $1,300, you can get a good quality racing bike with carbon forks. For $2,500 you are very much in the realm of a decent carbon-fiber bike with great gearing.

Of course you can go up from there but at this price range you can purchase a very good bike that will serve most of your career at a competitive level. For more money you are buying lighter components, smoother bearings, better absorption of road vibration, more precise gear shifting, increased braking power and some improved aerodynamic features.

You also need to consider whether you want a traditional racing bike or a more aerodynamic time trialing/triathlon shape bike. In general, for beginners the standard racing bike is best as it is more comfortable and can be used for sportives, longer casual rides, hills and racing.

Time trialing (TT) or triathlon bikes cost a lot more and can run into many thousands of dollars, so make sure you want to continue the sport before making this investment.

Also, the time trialing (TT) position is not so good for hills or turning corners. It is very much a race position. The longer the distance, the more this aerodynamic position counts.

If you are in your first season, do not even consider this type of bike. There is enough to get used to without an extreme cycling position as well.

If you are doing half Ironman or Ironman, this position will make a big difference over this length and you will see many more TT bikes on the course. Studies have shown there is approximately 22-24% energy saving comparing a road bike set up versus a full time trial bike with aero helmet set up. That equates to 5 minutes saved over 40km and a 25-minute saving over 180km.

As a compromise, many recreational triathletes simply clip aero bars onto their road bike to gain a bit of aerodynamic advantage whilst retaining the relative comfort and functionality of their road bike.

Body position

Your body position makes a huge difference to reducing drag and therefore riding faster.

A normal upright riding position versus an aero tuck position makes a difference of over 2 minutes over a 40km time trial on the bike. This is a massive advantage when you think that it may take you 2 months of hard training to improve by just 10 seconds on a time trial.

Comfort

Remember to consider comfort and fit. When you do buy a bike make sure you insist on the shop setting it up for you properly. You will be spending a lot of time on your bike and this will become a problem very quickly if you are not comfortable on it. A bike that is the wrong size for you will give you discomfort, pain and injury before long.

Nearly everything can be adjusted: handlebars height, seat height, type of seat, horizontal movement of seat. Spend the time to test these out and take some advice about them.

Equally, if you already have a bike that you have had for a few years, it is worth having a professional look at your position. As you improve as a cyclist, your position may change and adapt. You may be able to find an improved position.

Bike shoes

Proper cleats (where you clip your cycling shoe into the pedals) are very important and make a big difference in Olympic distances and above.

There is an argument for sprint distances about whether it is worth changing from cycling shoes to running shoes as the event is so quick. Some choose to just have toe clips and cycle in their running shoes; this enables them to simply jump off the bike and start running without a shoe change.

If you do decide to go for cleats, practice is essential as it can be tricky in the beginning clipping in and out of the bike. You just turn your heel out at the back on the side you wish to get off and unclip. Give yourself plenty of time in case it is a bit stiff at first. After a few goes it should become second nature and you won't have to think about it.

Make sure you practice running with your bike for a short distance with your shoes on and then hopping on, clicking in and riding away. You may want to try this on grass!

As you get more experienced, you can practice leaving your shoes in the pedals and putting them on as you ride away. For your first few races, however, if you wear trainers/ running shoes with toe clips there will be no need to worry about this.

Helmet

Wear a good quality helmet (many race organizers check this and ensure it meets certain safety standards). You are not allowed to race in a triathlon if you do not wear a helmet and it must be fastened BEFORE you get on your bike.

You will be disqualified if you take your bike off the rack and you do not have your helmet on. The best race practice is to put it on top of your bike so it is the first thing you do. When you come to return your bike to T2, leave your helmet on until you have racked your bike.

Most new helmets meet the safety standards, have good ventilation, and are light-weight. If you are doing Ironman distances, aero helmets have been shown to significantly reduce drag.

Reducing drag is the name of the game.

80-90% of resistance of forward momentum on the bike is aerodynamic drag and 70-75% of that is the rider!

"But aero helmets look silly. Is it worth it?"

An aero helmet will save to 60-90 seconds over a 40km time trial. That is significant and obviously multiplied for longer distances.

Wheels

Aero wheels make a massive difference. They reduce the watts you have to produce by 50 watts. Think how hard it is to achieve an extra 50 watts by training! But they come with a price tag.

Again, if you are a beginner do not even think about it - it's just something to keep in mind down the track.

Bike Computer

An important thing to have is a bike computer – Cat eye or Garmin, depending on your budget.

You should record accurate data about your mileage, average speed and time to add to your training diary. This can also provide you some real time motivation. For example, if there is a 40km ride you do every week and your usual average speed is 16km/hr, you will feel extremely proud of yourself if you do a hard ride and notice your average speed is now 17km/hr for the same ride, then in another month 18km/hr. Of course, allowances need to be made for wind resistance and so on but a good average gives you a guide of where you are.

Also, real time data can be important. So maybe there is a hill you normally climb in 42 seconds. Over the season, you may try to get that down to 35 seconds, then 29 seconds.

The Garmin-type computers now contain maps and GPS functions so you can plan your route in advance and don't have to stop every so often to consult maps. (This gets very awkward when it rains!). There are also programs you can add to allow you to compare an exact route you did against the time of your friends or other people in your club.

As well as keeping an accurate record of your training and race performances, bike computers are an awesome motivational tool.

Padded shorts

Padded cycling shorts are essential for comfort on the saddle with considerable padding to protect your delicate bits. But for race day, switch to tri shorts with less padding that you can wear for the swim, bike and run. This allows for faster transition as you will already be wearing everything you need and can just pull your wetsuit off and be ready to grab your bike and go.

Tri shorts usually have less padding than cycling shorts so it won't feel like you are wearing a wet nappy when you get on the bike!

Tri shorts are designed to be water repellant and seamless. Some of them also offer compressions fabric to reduce muscle fatigue.

Cycling gloves

Gloves are a highly recommended item for training, though most people don't bother with them in races because of the time it takes to put them on in transition. For training, however, cycling gloves make it more comfortable for your hands and wrists with a bit of padding and they are essential to protect your hands, if you ever come off the bike.

Superior Bike Technique

Believe it or not, there is quite a bit to cycling technique. Cycling will take up the majority of your training time. It also takes up the majority of the time in a race, so saving time here is very valuable.

Getting fast on the bike has two main components:

- Becoming as aerodynamic as possible
- Improving your strength and skill as a cyclist

The stronger you become at cycling, the more you will love it. The better your technique, the faster you will go with no extra training.

Most people do not consider bike technique at all. They just buy a bike and start pedaling.

Here are the key points to focus on in your next training ride:

1) Keep your upper body still (check your shadow to watch this).

Many cyclists move their back and their pelvis as they pedal. This eventually leads to back pain, knee pain and hip pain, and it not efficient. Instead, try to keep the upper body still and your core engaged.

Push from the legs and gluteal muscles (buttock) without engaging your back muscles. This will help you use all your energy on going forward, not wasting energy going side to side.

2) Relax your upper body.

This requires self-awareness. Many new cyclists are stiff in the arms and tense in the neck. Before long you will have aching neck and shoulders if this persists. As you become more comfortable on the bike, make a conscious effort to relax your hands and arms. Be aware of your neck area and relax it as well.

Neck, shoulder and wrist pain are very common among cyclists. Tensing your arms needlessly can become a bad habit.

Of course, there is a place in cycling for using your upper body - sprint finishes or difficult hill climbs, for example - but for the majority of the ride, continue to remind yourself to relax your upper body.

3) Rhythmic pedaling technique

If you cycle behind a beginner, then cycle behind a more advanced cyclist, you will notice a big difference between the two, even though both are just pumping up and down on the pedals.

There is smoothness and rhythm in a good cyclist's pedal technique that helps them apply smooth, even pressure to the pedals. Think about pedaling in a circular action with even power applied throughout the stroke. Many beginners just use an up and down motion and do not use their hamstrings at all. Instead, think of pushing down on one leg as you pull up with the other leg. Practice steady power and regular cadence throughout your ride.

Also, look ahead for hills and prepare gear changing in advance. This will allow you to maintain an even cadence rather than almost stopping and losing power before you have to scramble for the gears.

A usual "good" cadence for cyclists is thought to be around 90-100rpm. However, we must always keep in mind that cyclists are not triathletes and when they finish cycling they are finished.

Triathletes, however, have to run after they finish cycling - so do not copy everything from the world of cycling without adapting it slightly for our sport.

In triathlon, a slightly lower cadence is acceptable - around 75-85rpm. This will lead to lower lactate levels and allow better running off the bike. As you become more comfortable on the bike, you will get a feel for what is "normal' to you. As you progress, practice changing gears in anticipation of hills to maintain a similar cadence for most of the race.

You should also be able to reach down for your water bottle and drink while pedaling. Make sure you practice this in every training session. Continue to look forward, keep pedaling and drink when it is safe to do so as you will need this skill for the race.

If you have decided on aero bars, practice getting down on them and back up safely and with confidence.

There is quite a bit to focus on so make a list, then practice focusing on one aspect at a time.

Summary

- Scan your body as you ride.
- Upper body is relaxed.
- Expand your chest and breath deeply.
- Core is engaged.
- Power is generated from legs and gluteal muscles.
- Use a circular pedaling action.

Descending Fast

Non-cyclists would think that descending is the easiest thing in the world and is something that gives cyclists a "rest".

Actually, descending is when you need to sharpen your concentration and it can be extremely physical. A lot of cyclists hate descending as it can be quite scary and as a result a lot of cyclists lose speed, brake too often and get dropped by the group on the descents.

If you are a good descender, you will have a massive advantage. It involves confidence on the bike, good cornering skills, using your body weight effectively, managing your speed and picking your line well in advance.

Obviously, the more you practice descending and cornering, the better you will get, so seek many opportunities to practice.

Here are some things to think about to improve your technique and skill:

- Get down on the drops - this will lower your center of gravity, improve your handling and keep you more stable.
- Look out for bumps in the road, man-hole covers or loose gravel.
- Keep the skills you have learned – breathe, engage your core and relax your arms
- Sit slightly off the saddle if you can; this will give you natural suspension.
- Depending on the gradient, you may need to feather the brakes so you can control the speed. The worst thing you can do is suddenly brake; this could risk throwing you off. If you have someone close behind you, they may not be able to brake in time.
- When you go round a corner you should have you outside leg on the down pedal and the inside leg uppermost. This will enhance stability.
- Where you look is critical! The bike will go where you look! So look past the corner where you want to go. Never look at an obstacle (for example, a tree or a rock) or you are likely to head straight for it. Instead, look at the space between them or beyond them.
- Practice leaning the bike as you corner rather than turning

the handles bars.

- Similar to driving a car or riding a motorbike, try to avoid braking while cornering – this can cause you to skid or overbalance. Try to break BEFORE you get to the corner, then manage your speed through the corner.
- Anticipate the line you should take through the corner well in advance. When you are watching cycling like Tour de France or a triathlon, observe how they corner and watch the lines they take.

Remember, though, you may not often have the luxury of cycling without traffic so always consider safety first. You may need to brake more in case there is a car on the other side of the corner.

Drop The Pack: Ascending Magic

Climbing is also an important skill. It is not just about strength and fitness, though this certainly helps. Never avoid hills. I know plenty of cyclists who always opt for the flat ride where possible because "hills are hard."

This is crazy. Yes, hills are hard, and they will get you stronger, fitter, faster than your competitors in just a few weeks. Make sure you do some hill repeats every week. I have seen good cyclists who can drop the group on the flat almost come to a complete standstill as soon as an incline begins. It is incredible to watch. Climbing is a specific skill that needs to be practiced.

Practice standing in the saddle.

This is a great thing to do as it gives some of your muscles a rest while it uses other ones.

It also gives your back a break from constantly bending forward.

You will need to play around with your gearing as you will need a different gear if you are standing in the saddle versus spinning uphill in a seated position. Keep your core engaged and as the gradient increases, you will use more and more upper body effort to counterbalance your legs.

Get prepared mentally for ascending. If you approach it with dread, it will feel more difficult. Treat it with respect but know that you can do it. It is best to think about pacing, so rather than sprint up it and get exhausted (where you might never really recover for the rest of the race), just take it steady, keep breathing and use your gears.

Standing in the pedals takes more energy than sitting. So use it sparingly - on the last portion of the hill when your gears have run to is a good place to gain a bit more strength to get you to the top. Keep your chest open and keep breathing.

Practice hill reps often; your will be amazed how strong you get quite quickly.

Comfortable Bike Fit – Simple Tips

On a 60-minute ride you will probably spin your legs about 10,000 times. It is important you fit the bike correctly or you will soon feel knee strain and back pain. Also, a correct bike fit will allow you to perform better as your muscles will be in a more efficient position.

Here are the basics you can look at yourself. If you feel you need a more in-depth analysis, you will need to find a professional bike fit person who can apply computer readings to your limbs and work out the subtle tweaks you can make.

For most beginners, the advice below will suffice:

Frame size

Stand over the bike's top tube with both feet on the ground in your cycling shoes. There should be clearance of about 1 inch between the tube and your groin.

Saddle height

Your saddle height should be set so your legs are almost fully extend at the bottom of each pedal stroke but not fully extended and locked.

Saddle tilt

Saddle tilt is all about comfort. Try different positions and see what feels best. Slight upward tilt will relieve pressure on your sit bones. Slight downward tilt will reduce pressure on the front of your anatomy.

Handlebar position

If they are too low, your handlebars will make you bend over, further increasing strain on your back and neck. If they are too high, you will not be benefiting from aerodynamics as much as you could be.

Play around with this a little bit. It depends on whether or not you have a history of back or neck pain. The lower and flatter you are, the better for reducing drag. However, comfort is the most important thing as you will be spending many hours on your bike.

Cleat position

Misaligned cleats (shoes) may result in knee pain or back pain. Use trial and error to slightly loosen them and adjust them for the first few rides and see what feels right. Try to make sure your toes point forward, not in or out. Make sure your kneecaps point directly forward and tracks over your toes.

Make several adjustments and tweaks to your bike. Go for a ride and see how your feel. If you are not sure or you experience continual pain on the bike, get a professional bike fit. This will make all the difference.

Bike safety

Most of this section will be obvious but do NOT skip over it. It is very important to stay safe whilst you are training. There are many car drivers who are in a rush to get where they are going and they do not care about you, your bike or your life. They may be texting on their phone or just had a fight with their spouse. The sun may be in their eyes or there could be a hundred other reasons why they may not be paying attention. So assume everyone else can't see very well and take precautions.

Always wear a well-fitting helmet that meets the standards (you will need this for races anyway and the marshals are very strict about checking this).

Obey traffic signs and traffic lights.

If there is a bike lane, use it.

Wear bright reflective clothing, including bike gloves, which are a savior if you come off.

At night make sure you have bright lights front and back and carry spare batteries.

In the wet, wear waterproofs but, most importantly, slow down, especially on wet roads and when turning corners. Thin racing wheels are notorious for slipping out from underneath riders.

Be very careful when it has been wet, even if it is bright and sunny when you set out. Wet roads and wet leaves on roads can be a disaster waiting to happen.

It is better to be 1-2 minutes later than sprawled across the road with gravel rash cutting up your leg, a massive bruise on your hip or, even worse, a collarbone fracture. Take it easy on wet roads!

Group riding

Group riding is one of the most enjoyable parts of triathlon training. You are out with your buddies, enjoying the fresh air, enjoying a bit of banter and encouraging each other on. Group riding etiquette is very important for courtesy but also for safety.

Here is an overview of the common hand signals you should know and use:

If the group is coming to a stop, signal with your hand behind your back that you are stopping.

Also, when riding along, if you spot a pothole or other obstruction on the road, point it out to those behind you. Use hand signals to signal to traffic which way you are turning. When cyclists are riding behind each other, all one can see is the cyclist in front. So by the time they have suddenly slammed on the brakes, it is too late and accidents happen.

Signal early and make sure you help your fellow cyclists and they will feel inclined to help you. If out training with a small group, you may cycle two abreast. If you are riding on busy roads, ride single file. Always be courteous to drivers and they will usually be courteous to you.

If you are riding down a quiet road and see an oncoming car, shout to your fellow cyclists: "Car front!" so they are aware and will not try to overtake or speed up when it could be dangerous.

Shout: "Car back!" if you are at the back of the group and become aware of a car approaching you from behind to maintain the safety of the group.

Interval Training On The Bike

Interval training is the fastest way to improve on the bike. Consistent stressing of the body's lactate system is the key to achieving a faster race pace on the bike and a smoother transition from the bicycle to the run. You know when lactic build up is at threshold because your muscles ache, your breathing is rapid and your whole body is yelling at you to stop!

Lactic acid is produced in normal exercise as a waste product of muscle activity. When it is being produced faster than the body's ability to carry it away, you will experience the lactic burn that athletes dread.

Training at lactate threshold gets the legs used to this sort of pain and improves the body's ability to clear it quickly enabling you to cycle at higher intensities for longer. Instead of going for long steady state rides all the time, intersperse them with shorter, harder rides.

You will get fitter much faster by doing interval training than just doing comfortable steady state rides. It is also more realistic for racing.

For example, cycle easy for 10 minutes. Find a good, long road clear of traffic where possible and pedal as hard as you can for 2 minutes, then recover with gentle pedaling for 2 minutes. Repeat 5 times.

As your lactate tolerance increases, reduce the rest period and increase the workload. For example: pedal as hard as you can flat out for 3 minutes, recover 1 minute. Repeat 8 times.

For variety find some hills and do hill repeats. Stand up out of the saddle and sprint up the hill as fast as you can, then coast down. Repeat 10 times. These are the hard sessions that every athlete dreads but they are short and highly effective. They will make you super strong and fast-track your improvement.

Chapter 4:

What All Triathletes Should Know About Running Fast

Running is arguably the most technically difficult and the most demanding discipline on the body. But strangely, it is the one where most people think they can just get away with it because it is seemingly easy.

Why are so few people good runners?

Simple: cars, desk jobs, complacency and inactivity. Unless you have been part of the track team and kept running since you were a kid, it is likely you have quite a few underused muscles and have lost some flexibility.

Also, running is one activity that we do not think of getting "lessons" in until we are plagued with injury and finally realize that we MUST pay attention to our form, our stretching and our warm ups.

Even people who attend a running club are rarely schooled in "good form". Instead, the focus is on the workout. For example: whether you are doing 10 x 400s tonight or a couple of 5km efforts.

Running is one of the fastest ways to burn fat. This is good news but take care if you are overweight that you are not putting too much stress on your joints.

Learn to enjoy running but learn to do it right. It is the discipline of triathlon, which, if you do not get it right, will cause you the most amount of injuries and time off training.

Running fast happens through two mechanisms: improving fitness and strength and developing correct technique. If you ignore technique you WILL get injured - it will just be a matter of time.

The most common injuries with running are shin splints, Achilles pain and knee pain.

If you get one of these conditions, it can put you out of action for 6 weeks to 6 months, so take this seriously and get it right in the beginning.

Where to start?

Start conservatively. If you have not run before or not for a long time, start walking. This is very important if you are overweight. You are getting your joints and tendons ready for the pounding involved in running. When you are ready, add some jogging in between.

For example: run/walk for 20 minutes. Keep building the distance but never more than 10% increase week to week.

Gradually build up to running 3-4 times a week, 30-40 minutes, then add one longer run a week if you are training for the longer distances.

Always listen to your body. If it needs an extra day off running, allow it. This does not mean skipping training. It means switching that session to swimming, cycling or a core work out.

What About The Treadmill?

Often runners and triathletes state that they "never training indoors" and hate gyms. However, the treadmill does have its place!

The disadvantages are obvious:

We race outside, so we should train outside in the same conditions.

When we run outside, we learn to propel our body forward with our own force instead of relying on the treadmill to do it and simply try to "keep up".

The advantages are numerous:

If you are a new runner, the treadmill provides more cushioning and is easier on your joints than if you run outside. Having a treadmill with a mirror in front of you is awesome for getting visual feedback of how your posture is when you are running and your leg and body alignment.

If you see a leg kicking out to the side, or your hips swinging wildly from side to side, try to make small corrections. This is invaluable feedback.

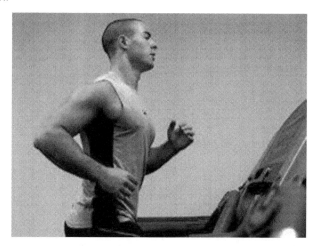

You can do some pretty serious hill repeats on the treadmill and get an awesome workout in a short space of time. You can do some fantastic speed workouts and be very objective about your speed and time. Treadmills are brilliant for those wet, rainy, cold days that are unpleasant or icy. Sometimes it is dangerous to go out and hit the pavements.

It also makes for an extremely efficient workout - one that you could fit in before or after work, or at lunchtime. For the time pressed athlete (most of us) we can get amazing benefits from regular short 20-30 minute treadmill sessions as opposed to waiting until we have time to get a 3 hour run in (then over-doing it).

Of course, it is not wise to do ALL your training indoors but once or twice a week provides a different scene and allows you to focus on technique and form.

Good running form

I will go through some of the most important points of running so you have something to focus on and practice when you are thinking about your technique:

If possible, have someone video your gait and give you some pointers.

You will learn so much from looking at yourself run. Sadly, even though we may feel like Usain Bolt or Michael Johnson when we run, we look somewhat different!

Here I will summarize the main points of running technique, which will give you a major advantage when you are training and trying to get your gait sorted.

Think about:

- Running tall
- Leaning forward slightly
- Landing on the balls of your feet
- Minimizing upper body movement
- Relaxing your arms and shoulders
- Steady breathing
- Strong gluteal muscles
- A stable core

Do not build up the mileage too quickly – no more than 10% a week.

Schedule in a combination of short interval sessions and longer steady state runs.

Listen to your body. If it has considerable pain, rest it for a day or two. The worst thing you can do is "push through the pain", then require 6 weeks or more off because of shin splints or some other running injury.

Strong gluteal muscles

This point is so important that it needs fleshing out.

The muscles in your backside are THE running muscles. The glutes are the muscles in your bottom, the muscles you sit on all day. They *should be* the strongest muscle in your body.

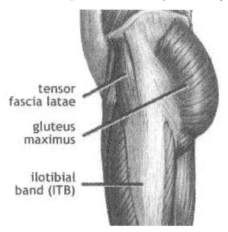

tensor fascia latae

gluteus maximus

ilotibial band (ITB)

But in many runners, they are the weakest.

If you tend to sit for most of the day at work, the glutes "forget" what they are meant to do and other muscles start to compensate, like the hamstrings or the lower back.

If these smaller muscles are over-working and compensating for weak, inactive glutes, this may be one reason you always get back ache when you run or always have tight hamstrings.

The glutes are a major hip extensor. It is from here you should be generating your power and forward momentum when you run. The glutes also help stabilize the pelvis and keep your core solid so you do not lose energy.

As you get stronger glutes, your running will dramatically improve and your injury rate will dramatically reduce!

Exercise:

Squats, lunges and dead lifts are the key exercises to ensuring your gluteal muscles are active, strong and ready to run.

Add these in to your program every week (more about strength training later).

Do 3 x 8 reps. Start with body weight only, progress to dumbbells or a bar bell when ready.

Shoes and laces

The main difference in shoes these days is how much heel and cushioning they have. For the longer runs – half marathon and above – a bit of cushioning is wise. For shorter runs, the lighter the shoe, the better.

Definitely get your trainers from a good running shoe store that can take a quick video of your gait and steer you in the direction of neutral shoes versus anti-pronation shoes. Talk to them about your event and your distance and they will be able to advise you specifically.

If you can find comfortable shoes get speed laces so you can just pull them on and go without worrying about tying laces. If not, prepare your shoes before the race starts so it takes you minimal time to lace your shoes up. Do not buy new shoes 1-2 weeks before your event. Definitely train in them, making sure you do not feel blisters or rubbing points anywhere.

Also, there is the sock argument. Many triathletes do not wear cycling or running socks on race day, again to assist minimizing transition time. The longer the race, the more likely it is that athletes wear socks. Whatever you decide to do, make sure you practice it several times in training first!

Pacing yourself

Pacing is an important discipline in racing. Too many athletes get over-excited in a race. They start running too quickly, then "blow up" and have to "shuffle" or "limp" the last few miles.

In training, get to know your comfortable steady-state pace. If possible, buy yourself a GPS watch or similar device, which will tell you what your pace is in real time.

The most important metric is the average pace for the whole run. The purpose of a GPS watch or similar is as much to hold you back at the beginning of a run as it is to keeping an eye on your time.

From knowing what your pace is, you can design specific training programs. For example, you might run 10km at 8min/mile pace. So you might do an interval session 4 x 400m sprints at 6min/mile pace. This is teaching your body to run at a faster pace, your legs to turn over faster, your breathing to adapt to this pace and your energy systems to get used to clearing out lactic acid faster and delivering you more energy.

Running faster

The only way to learn to run faster is to practice running faster!

Pretty obvious, right?

But, no! This one never fails to amaze. So many runners run their same routes at the same speed at the same time week in, week out.

And guess what?

They never improve their times from year to year.

Of course they are staying healthy and it is better than sitting on the sofa but they often get frustrated that they are putting in all this time and seeing no results.

The secret is simple.

You MUST run faster in training.

Try interval training. There are many ways to do this.

Make sure you warm up first, then sprint a certain distance, then recover a certain distance, then sprint, then recover for a certain time period.

So, an example would be sprinting to the next telegraph pole, then jogging to the next one, then sprinting to the next one and so on. If you have access to a track, a great workout is to sprint 200m, then jog 200m.

Repeat 8-10 times.

Or you could do it by time. Look at your watch. Sprint 20 seconds, then jog 10 seconds, sprint 20 seconds, jog 10 seconds.

**Do an interval session at least once a week
of 25-50 minutes and you WILL see a dramatic
improvement in your time-guaranteed!**

You should also enter local 5km races. These are great for developing your speed and race experience and will also get you used to running with other people.

Hill repeats also have the same effect of improving your speed, your strength and your cardiovascular fitness in a short space of time. Simply find a hill, run up it as fast as you can, then jog or walk back down. As you get better, increase the number of repeats and find longer hills to run.

The message here is to really mix it up. Do not get stuck in a routine of doing a slow plod every time you put your trainers on.

By the way, hill repeats and sprints will really improve your upper body strength and your core, which is great for the longer distances. When you fatigue in the upper body or core, your running form begins to suffer and running becomes a lot harder.

Interval training means you can get a lot done in a small amount of time without spending hours and hours plodding at the same speed.

What is the difference between good pain and bad pain?

That is a great question and one that every runner should think about and be prepared for. More runners get injured every year than in any other sport even though it is a non contact sport. This is mainly due to over training and poor biomechanics!

Remember your rest periods – you cannot train all the time. Good running technique is important as is learning to listen to your body. The advantage of doing triathlon instead of just running is you become a much better all-round athlete. You have more balanced muscle development and you mix up your training with other movements besides just pounding the streets.

When you are fatigued, you are more likely to get injured because your form goes. So when this happens, ease up on the distance or the intensity for a few days until you feel better. Seriously, it is much better to have a couple of easier days training than develop shin splints or Achilles tendonitis and have to endure 6 weeks off training. This will drive you insane!

Most people do not realize it until it happens. They think they are invincible. They think it won't happen to them. They keep pushing through the pain, thinking they can train through it and the pain will just go away. But guess what? It doesn't!

Be smart, listen to your body and rest when it needs it, and push hard when you are feeling good.

You will have days when you have pushed hard, when you feel fatigued and feel "good pain". Your lungs are burning. Your legs feel heavy. You feel like you can't go on.

The process of being an athlete involves pushing your body to the point where it gets tiny muscles tears (this is the muscle soreness you sometimes feel after training). The muscle then repairs itself and grows stronger. This is necessary for improvement.

Bad pain and too much fatigue occur when your form changes. You alter your stride in some way because every step is almost impossible, or you experience sharp pain with every step.

This is definitely time to listen!

Sometimes all you need is a couple of days off. Your body will heal and recover. You will come back stronger. If you keep pushing at this point, your hamstring tweak may develop into a full-blown tear, which means 6 weeks off.

Or your sniffle and raised heart rate will develop into flu and glandular fever and you may need 3 months off and your season is over, gone, finished!

Learn this lesson now – do not learn the hard way.

Plan your week

In general, you should not increase your training volume and intensity in the same session. Choose one. Remember to mix up your training speeds. Sometimes do long, slow runs. Sometimes choose shorter, hard intervals sessions. Do not choose hard, long runs especially in the beginning. It is not worth it.

Remember the 10% rule!

Sometimes in the beginning you can get away with it. For example, if you can only run 2 miles, then increase to 4 miles. That is usually ok because the training volume is low anyway. But you would not go from running 10 miles one week, to running 8 miles 3 times the next week because that would total 24 miles and a crazy increase of 240%. It would not be long before your body would break down with injury.

So set out a sensible training program.

Keep a training journal of how you are feeling each week. Adjust it if you have to.

The mistake a lot of marathon runners and triathletes make is they set out their training plan but mid way through they get injured and need 3-4 weeks off. Obviously, they will have missed a lot of training runs. They either jump straight back into the week they should be on or they add in extra runs trying to do all the mileage they missed according to the program and overloading their systems straight away. This is a guaranteed way to end up back on the physical therapist's couch!

Normal training pain is usually generalized ("oh, my legs hurt today") rather than localized ("oh, there is sharp, localized pain in my knee"). Definitely have a couple of days off if you experience localized pain in the same spot for more than a couple of sessions in a row. If the pain has not gone after a couple of days rest, seek professional help. If you get it seen quickly, the problem usually resolves itself quickly.

Essential Running Drills

There is more about running to keep in mind than just the feet! In fact, the more I learn and experience about running, the less and less it is about the feet, and the more it is about the core, the overall posture, the arms and what is going on inside my head. The feet are simply a by-product that will behave perfectly well if everything else is doing what it should be doing.

Running is a very technical sport and to get good at it, you need to break it down into its components and practice each one.

All good runners do drills – no exceptions!

It is important to get the basics right or you will start to notice niggles and injuries more frequently.

Here are a couple of easy drills that will make a big difference to your running times.

Drill 1

Most people do not bend their knee up at the back when they run. If you look at good runners they have a high knee lift at the front and at the back of their swing cycle.

This requires less distance for the leg to travel. This results in a higher cadence and less fatigue and means you will run faster.

Heel-to-butt kicks. During your normal run, begin to exaggerate knee flexion, touching the butt with the heel during each stride. Do 20 touches for both the right and left legs, then continue in your normal gait pattern.

Drill 2

Single knee bends. Most people struggle with this one. Stand on one leg and bend your knee. Watch your knee in a mirror if possible and make sure it travels directly forward.

80% of people will notice either:

- They can't balance on one leg or
- Their knee drifts inwards

If either of these things happen you will be losing energy and may be at risk of getting runner's knee due to the adverse forces at the knee joint.

The drill involves practicing this skill.

Do 3 x 15 reps twice a day.

If you think about it, running is actually a series of one knee bends done fast!

Practice this many times - this is a fundamental skill of running. If you can't balance on one leg you will have running problems. If you can't bend your knee keeping your knee straight, you will have running problems.

Drill 3

Cadence counts. During your run, count the number of right foot strikes achieved in a span of 20 seconds. There should be 30 or more, indicating a cadence of 90 or higher. Increased cadence indicates decreased ground contact time.

Remember to stay light on your feet and think about relaxation as you run. This will reduce fatigue and make you a faster runner.

Summary

Remember to stay relaxed and stay mentally focused while you are running. Practice good form all the time.

Practice does not make perfect – perfect practice makes perfect.

Do not get stronger at the wrong thing!

Chapter 5:

Lightning Quick Transitions

Transition is unique to multi sport events. Even if you are good at running, cycling and swimming, if you cannot get through transition very well, you will lose a lot of time. If you get it wrong, you risk disqualification. Many call transition "the fourth discipline" as it is a skill that MUST be practiced to make it streamlined, effortless and give you a competitive advantage.

Transition 1 (T1) is the transition from swim to bike and transition 2 (T2) is from bike to run. Most people think they will "wing it" on the day and they end up getting flustered, making mistakes and losing valuable time.

It does not make sense to get up at 5am every day to train before work to shave a minute off here and a minute off there and then waste 10 minutes in transition!

**Transition is a source of valuable "free" time
if you practice it.**

Most people won't practice it – so here is a valuable place you can sneak up the rankings!

Remember, the clock does not stop. So you want to get in and out of there as fast as you can WITHOUT getting flustered or sending your heart rate through the roof!

The transition area is also one of the likeliest area for crashes. Athletes are in a hurry, there is water around on slippery mats from the swim and people tend to take risks.

So be systematic, have a plan and be focused.

How Often To Practice

As with most things, preparation and practice is essential. This one tip alone will save you many minutes, much anguish and even possible disqualification. Some athletes tell me they practice transitions. When I drill down, it turns out that they only practice the week before a race.

I'm afraid this is not enough.

Transition is a particular skill and can gain you so many minutes; it is worth practicing every week. You need it to become automatic. Sometimes things seem easy in training but in a race situation, stress may make you forget. You need it on autopilot so you don't have to think.

Practice your transitions every week. Do not wait until the day before the race to think what you need or you will be sure to forget something. Many triathletes wait until the night before the race when the shops are closed to think through what they need on race day.

If they have forgotten anything - extra gels, spare inner tubes or Vaseline - it will be too late. Or they will lie awake all night wondering if they should find a late night convenience store or hope and pray there will be a stall selling supplies at the venue.

It's just not worth it.

The stress of race day is enough even when you are totally prepared without adding the stress of getting by without your extra gel or praying you won't puncture as you only brought one spare inner tube.

Your weekly practice

Most people won't do this!

Think every week about the most efficient way to move from swim to bike (T1) and bike to run (T2). Practice it lots of times physically and also rehearse it lots of times mentally. By the time race day comes you should be on autopilot.

No clutter. Be as minimalist as possible. Get rid of any steps you don't need, like socks or gloves. Get in and out fast! At least once a week, when you plan a ride, also plan to come back and run straight away so you are practicing the transition as well.

Think about what you need and set it up so when you come back you keep your watch on, rack your bike, helmet off, sun hat on, change your shoes, grab an extra gel if you need one or a sip of water and head straight off.

Over the course of a few months, write down what you need and start to create a list of what you need for race day, what gels suit you, how much water you need for the run, if you need a hat and sun glasses, if you prefer the same bike socks and run socks, if you prefer to change socks, or if you prefer no socks.

It is important to sort out all these things along the way.

Also, make sure you do them systematically, in the same order, each and every time.

So when you come home with the bike, take off your helmet and bike shoes in the same way and put on your run shoes and socks, sun hat and whatever other change you are making in the same way. Do it the same every time. Then, in the pressure cooker situation of race day transition, you don't have to think about it. It happens automatically as you have done it so often before.

My friend Matt did not bother practicing transition. He took the easy option of "just running through it" in his head the night before. On race day, he came back into T2 with his bike and he unstrapped his helmet as he was running to his bike rack. He got an instant DQ! Disqualification - no questions asked. Of course he knew that rule of not taking your helmet off until you rack the bike - he had done other races before - but because it was not programmed into his subconscious, he forgot for an instant and that was the end of his day.

Do not let this happen to you.

To be specific for anyone who does not know: race rules mean you must ALWAYS have your helmet on in transition. Do not start cycling without your helmet on. Do not even run with your bike until you have your helmet on. You may be instantly disqualified. Marshalls take this very seriously. Put your helmet on your bike. Put it on first and strap it up before you do anything else. When you come back off the bike leg into transition 2 (T2), make sure you keep your helmet on until the bike is securely racked in its correct spot. Take it off last.

By the way, racking your bike securely both at the beginning of the race and in T2 is important. I have seen occasions where other athletes have knocked off neighboring bikes in the rush to get going fast.

Do you think they stopped to pick up the bike they knocked over?

Can you imagine the turmoil you would be in when you return to your beloved bike and you see it crashed to the floor and athletes running over it in the rush to the exit?

Plan Your Mat Lay Out Like A Winner

Lay out your transition area out a few times during the season and run through both transitions including full "costume change" and time them. Again, be very systematic about your lay out - do the same thing every time. There is nothing worse than fumbling about looking for something that you forgot to lay out, having to dive into your bag and get all your dry clothes wet or simply wasting time.

So here is a suggestion. Try this or develop your own system that works for you. Remember, it is a system so once you have thought about it and tested it a few times, make sure you lay it out the same way, every time. You will place a transition towel or transition mat next to your bike. Try using a bright, distinctive towel to help in spotting your area. This will help you identify your bike but also it is something to dry your feet with when you come into T1.

Face your towel/mat. Place your race belt and shoes at the top. Make sure that the tongue of your shoes and laces are open to make it as easy as possible to get your feet in and out. Place your bike shoes on the towel directly behind your running shoes. Loosen up the straps and make sure they are open and ready to place your feet in them. Most of the time, competitors don't wear socks with shoes on the bike or the run. However, if you choose to wear socks, place the socks ready to put on in the shoes so they are exactly where you need them.

Your race belt with your race number for the bike and run should be placed under your bike shoes. This keeps the race number from blowing away and reminds you to put it on when you put your shoes on. (Another way of doing this is to put your race belt under your wet suit so you don't have to worry about it or put it on in transition).

Some competitors will safety pin their race number on their shirt, but if it starts flapping on the bike it can be very irritating, so it is wise to use a race belt. Race belts can be purchased for about three dollars from most stores that stock tri gear.

Leave the portion of the towel to the rear of your bike and closest to you open to stand on when you arrive. The reason you do this is because as you exit the swim and come into the transition area, you will have dirt, sand, grass and small rocks on your feet. Wipe your feet as you arrive.

Also, place a water bottle near this area so that you can wash away any debris you pick up. Depending on the venue, it may be a good idea to have a bucket of water at your transition area as well. For example, if it is a beach venue, you will be running up the sand. Cycling or running with sandy feet will give you a nasty blister for sure! So dunk your feet in, quickly towel dry and you will be set!

After you initially locate everything, make sure you know where all your hydration is located for the race. If it is going to be a particularly hot day, bury your running cap in the bottom of an ice chest so it will be nice and cold and give you some assistance in bringing your core temperature down.

Place your helmet on your bike bars and put your shades (if you are going to wear some) inside. This serves as a reminder to put your helmet on before you touch the bike.

Your hydration should already be on your bike, ready to go. Most athletes use the general rule of one bottle filled with sports drink and one bottle filled with water. It will depend on your distance how much water or sports drink you require.

For half Ironman and Ironman distance, you will also have aid stations with fuel every 5 miles or so; make sure you have researched this. Make sure you know where they are and what they are offering. Also, make sure you have tested out their brand to ensure it agrees with you. The length of your race will determine if you need food or not. If you do - you can tape some energy gels or bars to the bike.

Some other things to remember are:

- Reset your bike computer before the race.
- If you use a heart rate monitor, have your strap strapped around your bike so you can quickly put it on.
- Double-check to make sure your bike is in the right gear (you need to be on your small chain ring in front and a gear that you can easily push coming out of Transition One).

Remember to practice both transitions in training several times - well in advance!

The swim-bike transition may be more tricky for some people. If you train in a pool, it is unlikely you usually swim in a wetsuit. But do not get to race day without practicing getting out of a wet wetsuit! So swallow your pride and try the wet suit in the pool once or twice (you will have cap and goggles on so no one will recognize you!).

It is a very different beast to getting out of dry wetsuit!

This happened to me and I went dizzy with the effort of getting out of my wet wetsuit even though I had practiced the dry wetsuit routine many times!

So if you have access to open water or a lake it should be fairly easy to swim in a wet suit. Then have your bike on the back of the car or chained up close by.

How to Get Through Transition Faster

Many athletes new to triathlon see the transition area as a place to regroup, rest, chat and get their gear together. WRONG!

This is a place where you can gain serious competitive advantage over your competitors.

The clock does not stop while you are in there; every second extra adds to your race time!

How many hours of training will it take you to knock 2 minutes off your swim time? Probably hundreds or thousands of training hours.

How many hours will it take to knock 2 minutes off your transition time?

Probably one hour of practice!

Practice will also help you use the least amount of energy possible and keep your heart rate low.

Strategy 1: Bike shoes in pedals

I will discuss some advanced techniques. If this is your first triathlon, do not do this for your first race. I am putting it here so you know about it and it is something to consider down the track.

If you have decided to go with bike shoes, the fastest way to go through T1 is to leave your bike shoes already clipped into the pedals. Starting with them on the bike will get you going much quicker than others who are sitting down putting on their shoes.

As you approach T1, start taking your wetsuit off. It should be down at your waist by the time you reach your bike. Then pull it down to your ankle sin one go. Then 2 seconds to get each leg out of the wetsuit.

Put on your helmet straight away so you do not forget. Add sunglasses if you use them and dry your feet on the towel.

All your nutrition and hydration should be on the bike already.

Put on your race belt unless it is already on.

Run with your bike to the exit, then jump on your bike and start pedaling with your feet on top of the shoes until you get to cruising speed, then slip your feet into the shoes.

Keep your eyes on the road at all times, not on your feet. You will have gained good time on other athletes. This is not a beginner's technique but if you are a few seasons in and feeling confident, try it many times in practice.

As you return from the bike leg and approach T2, slip your feet out of the shoes, keep pedaling and then, before the line, swing your leg over so you can run straight away into transition. Practice this many times beforehand so you are confident.

Keep your helmet on until you rack your bike.

In T2, run with your bike while holding the seat. Practice this in a parking lot well in advance.

I am serious.

Triathletes sometimes crash in T2 as the handlebars swerve to the side, causing the athlete to slip or run into someone else.

I have even seen professionals make the same mistake.

Take care that you do not cut your shins on the pedals.

As I said above, everything you need on the bike course should be attached to your bike. Gel should be taped to the frame, water bottles should already be on board, spare tube in a seat pack and a CO_2 cartridge taped to the seat post.

Strategy 2: Bike rack awareness

Have you ever returned to a car park and had trouble finding your car?

You can have a similar experience in a large transition area (that is, unless you are last out, when your bike will be the only one left).

If you are in the middle of the pack it can be very disorientating with everyone rushing around you. Note carefully where your rack spot is and how to find it from the swim exit and bike entrance.

Strategy 3: Transition area "walk through"

Get to the race early, rack your bike and do a "walk through".

Start where the swim exit is, note a landmark to find your bike quickly (for example, 3rd row back in front of the flagpole). Walk to your bike, visualizing the race and people rushing past you. Visualize your quick change and then walk to the exit of T1.

Then find out where the T2 entrance is walk in from there and picture racking your bike, super quick changeover for the run and heading out of the T2 exit.

This won't take long and will pay massive dividends and you know exactly where the entrances and exits are. Sometimes triathletes assume they know from the pre race information but often it looks very different when you are at the venue.

The more you know, the less risk you have of being shouted at by an official that you are going the wrong way and getting flustered!

Strategy 4: Extras: Speed laces, spares and baby powder

Tying your running-shoe laces in a bow takes time. Eliminate this step by using lace locks or speed laces. Better still, have elastic ones so you don't need to tie them at all. To help your feet slide smoothly into your running shoes, prime them with a sprinkling of baby powder.

The other advantage of lace locks is that there is less risk of your shoe laces coming undone. There is nothing worse than wasting time tying shoe laces - and even worse doing this twice if the laces come undone during your run!

I also favor leaving a spare pair of sunglasses on my transition mat. Sometimes I use the same sunglasses that I use for cycling. But if it is a long race, my sunglasses may be covered in sweat, dirt and bugs so I like to have a fresh pair for the run. It be may be psychological but it makes me feel like I am fresher!

Depending on which tires you use, make sure you have spare inner tubes and a small light-weight pump or CO_2 cartridge. This is obvious but make sure whichever method you use that you have practiced it. I am constantly amazed at athletes who have switched to the CO_2 system but have never tried it out! They say they have never had a flat tire so have not had a chance to practice it.

The golden rule is:

Never do anything in the race that you have not done several times in practice!

In your transition practice you do need to be sure you can change a tire quickly under pressure in less than 2 minutes. Some people can do it in less than 1 minute.

I have watched some people in despair take over 10 minutes!

Always be focused on eliminating too many steps and reducing clutter. Try to minimize the risk of things that could go wrong.

Strategy 5: Mental rehearsal

Mental rehearsal is something you can do little and often to lay down neural pathways and to help your brain remember the sequence. When you picture things vividly, the brain can't distinguish between reality and vivid mental rehearsal. Transition is a brilliant thing to picture mentally for 5 minutes each day.

Picture every detail as vividly as possible.

When you do this the first time, have a piece of paper nearby to write down everything you need in two columns for T1 and T2. As you get more familiar with it you should not need to write much - only add the occasional thing that you may have forgotten.

Check your race list many times and laminate it.

I have known people to get to a race and forget their wetsuit, their bike or their ID. (Not the same person, I hasten to add) But it is easy to do.

So prepare this stage thoroughly. Do not simply pray and hope it be OK on the day. Make sure of it.

Chapter 6:

Training Secrets of The Pros

This chapter will discuss two incredible training strategies that most newbies don't do.

And many intermediates rarely do.

They both give you amazing results for very little time spent. And if you do them in the beginning of your triathlon journey, you will progress far more quickly than your contemporaries.

Strategy 1: Brick sessions

Brick sessions refer to training two disciplines during the same workout.

Bricks are a very important part of triathlon (and duathlon) training and they are sometimes overlooked. The two disciplines should be trained one after the other with minimal or no interruption in between, just as you would do in a race.

It is NOT enough just to train the three sports separately throughout the week - they MUST be put together and trained back to back.

Brick sessions may refer to a bike/run workout, a swim/bike workout or a run/bike workout (if you are training for a duathlon).

Many people ignore these, knowing it is something they "should" do. But if they do not schedule it in their plan, it simply never gets done!

Chrissie Wellington, four time World Ironman champion, credits brick sessions as THE most important session of her week! She did brick sessions EVERY week. She acknowledged that she was not the fastest individual swimmer, cyclist or runner. At any one sport she would have been beaten, but put them all together and she was the best.

So schedule it and do it!

It does not have to take a massive amount more time.

If the major focus of your day is to get a 40-mile bike in, focus on that and you may choose to do a 15-minute run on the end. You don't have to always follow with a 10-20km run!

Brick sessions will teach you so much:

- Your legs to run well off the bike
- Give you mental confidence
- Reduce the risk of "jelly" legs
- Give you physical confidence and certainty that you can do it well as you will have done it so many times
- Help you identify the correct nutrition for you so you don't risk stomach cramps on the run through too much fluid or incorrect fuel on the bike
- Help you master transitions as you practice your bike-run routine or swim-bike routine
- Reduce risk of leg cramps
- Help you understand the perfect pacing for your bike leg so you have enough "left in the tank" for the run

Swim/bike brick

While you are swimming a lot of the blood will be in your shoulders and arms so when you stand up on land, the blood tends to rush towards your legs, causing you to feel faint or giddy.

So start kicking your legs hard for the last 50-100meters of the swim to get the blood in your legs so you are not stumbling around or have to sit down for a minute until you get your bearings.

A swim/bike workout that simulates race conditions will help you minimize this problem.

Always start your bike leg using an easier gear than the one you plan on using during the main part of the race. This will give your legs a chance to get used to the new sport and accumulate less lactic acid than they would if you started from the beginning with a tough gear.

Logistically, some people train at a pool and can have the bike chained up outside. Some people train at a gym pool where they can go quickly inside and jump on a spin bike or turbo trainer set up by the pool.

Obviously, if you have the chance to swim in open water with a wetsuit, do this to practice the transition specifically.

Here are some examples of swim/bike brick sessions:

Sprint distance: 200 meter swim and 15 minute bike at 80-90% max heart rate (MHR)

Olympic: 400 meter swim followed by 25 minute bike at 80% MHR

Half Ironman: 2000 meter swim followed by 2 hour bike ride at 80% MHR

Ironman: 3000-4000 meter swim followed by 2-3 hour bike ride at 75% MHR

These are just guidelines for workouts.

Sometimes you won't have time to do these longer sessions, but even if you can do one of the disciplines properly then bolt on 10-15 minutes of the second discipline you will get valuable transition practice in and continue to remind your body that there will be something more to come.

Little and often is much better than doing it all at once the week before the event!

You can also add in repeats for variety such as:

3 x (500 meter swim + 5 mile bike).

This is more useful and time-efficient than doing a 1,500 meter swim followed by a 15 mile bike, because you will switch sports 6 times instead of only once.

Bike/run bricks

These are more important mainly because the transition between bike and run is the tougher of the two during a triathlon. There are two reasons for this:

1. You are using largely similar muscle groups.
2. You are already a long way through the race so you will already be exhausted and energy depleted.

Most people's recount of their brick workouts consist of a medium/long bike ride followed by a medium run.

Although these kinds of bricks are great, another recommendation is a sequence of short/medium rides alternated with a series of short runs.

Here are a couple of bike/run examples:

Sprint triathlon workout: 8-10km bike + 2km run at 75% MHR - repeat three or four times.

Or

Try this one: a 15 minute cycle at the hardest threshold you can maintain followed by a 10 minute run (5 minutes at threshold and 5 minute sprint with anything you have left)

Olympic triathlon workout: 70 minute bike followed by a 45 minute run at 75% MHR

Or

Strength brick: Cycle a 30 minute hilly course or hill repeats, followed by 10 minute running hill repeats.

By doing a series of short repeats you also switch sport (and therefore muscles used) several times in the same workout. You are teaching your legs and body to switch as fast as possible and as efficiently as possible between two very different kinds of effort.

Again, consider a series of short repeats. These are very efficient, especially when you are short on time.

<u>Ironman or half Ironman distance</u>: 60 minute cycle followed by 90 minute run

It may be difficult to fit this in every week if you already do a long run and a long ride. If you are struggling for time, switch this for your long run. It is more important to learn to run with bike fatigue in the legs.

As race day approaches, start to put all three together.

1000m hard swim followed by a 5km 90% MHR cycle followed by a 3km 90% MHR run.

(Increase the distances for the Ironman)

If you have never done a brick before, you should get used to them gently before attempting the kind of workouts described above.

Start with a 1km jog or jog/walk after every bike ride. You can start by walking briskly when you get off the bike and then move to a jog or run within 1km.

You can also attempt your first brick by biking in the morning and then running in the afternoon or after a 1 to 2 hour break.

When you stop biking and start running your legs may feel "strange" and heavy and the heart rate goes up as the body tries to switch the blood from flowing into the muscles used for cycling to those used for running.

This feeling is more pronounced at the start of the run and usually the legs get better as time passes, although never as fresh as when you run without biking beforehand.

Brick workouts help shorten the time your legs take to adapt, thus allowing you to run better and faster. It is not uncommon to experience cramps when starting to run after biking, especially if you are not used to it.

As usual, listen to your body and slow down if you feel a cramp coming. Gel and water will help if you are experiencing cramps due to the decrease in muscle fuel.

Strategy 2: Strength training

Do not dismiss strength training as just for bodybuilders fixated on their own reflection. Strength training will make a huge difference to your training as well as race performance and will also help improve your technique, stamina and prevent injury. It will also improve your resistance to lactic acid build-up.

We all know triathlon is a great endurance sport. We train for hours to refine and enhance our stamina and our ability to keep going at a steady pace for long periods of time.

In the beginning most triathletes spend as much time as possible on the bike, swim and run to gain experience and endurance. This is proper and correct.

However, as you advance in your training, the quickest way to get faster and better is through gaining strength as well. You will be so grateful for some strength on hilly courses when others are failing on the hills and you can easily overtake them, on a windy day when you cut through the wind resistance like a knife or at a critical point in the race when it counts; you can accelerate and go with the lead bunch, or make a break or sprint to the finish line faster than your friend.

Strength gives you such a significant advantage that I add it to every triathlon-training program I design because it is that important. It is also a massive advantage because most triathletes do NO strength training whatsoever so if you do, you will be miles ahead and make progress more quickly without getting injured.

So, if it is so good, why isn't every triathlete doing strength work?

These are the common excuses:

- "It will make me bulky and therefore slower."
- "I don't have time."
- "I don't know exactly what to do to be effective."

These are all false reasons for not doing strength training.

The excuse of not knowing what to do is easy to overcome. Get a trainer to spend one hour with you to show you the basics and check your technique. You will be safer and it will stop you from looking like a newbie. In fact, some of the strengthening work can be done at home with no equipment or very simple pieces of equipment.

So even if you are a gym-hater, there is no need to throw strength training out the window. Just do it at home.

Strength training does not have to make you bulky. You can train in a way that gives you enormous strength but does not make you huge and bulky.

Triathletes are always struggling with finding enough time to fit in all three sports. Substituting one or two sessions a week for a half-hour gym session will add more time in your life, not take it away. You will get far more benefit by doing a 30-40 minute strength session than simply going for just another 2 hour ride or run.

And another bonus: you will experience
far less risk of injury!

90% of triathletes experience injury at some point that puts them out of training for several weeks. Many of these injuries are preventable.

Strength training not only strengthens your muscles but also your joints, ligaments and tendons, making you more resilient to injury. Of course, the exercises must be specific to triathlon and not just general strength training and that is what I am going to cover in this chapter.

When you think about athletes from each of the three separate sports, they all do strength training – swimmers, cyclists and runners.

They do it to enhance the muscles they need to improve performance but they also do it to maintain muscle balance, which enhances race results and prevents injury.

Cyclists and runners spend many hours a week doing squats, lunges and leg presses. Even though they cycle or run hard at least 2 sessions a day, they still do strength training on top of that.

Swimmers do lots of shoulder and back strength work. And they all do core-strengthening as an essential; even though they train hard for 4 hours a day in the pool they still do added strength training.

Many triathletes say they just use the bike or the pool as their strength training. Whilst you can do functional resistance training on the bike or in the pool, you still need to do strength exercises separately to work the muscles that get under utilized when you swim, bike or run.

It does not have to take long; 30-40 minutes at a time is all you need to experience noticeable improvements.

Starting out

If you have never done strength training before, start very light. You need to get your body used to the movements and you do not want to get injured. Be consistent. Once a week is ok, twice a week is better, but once every three or four weeks is not.

If you go to the gym, great! Many triathletes do it on the same day as their swim session if they are already at the gym. This saves time. If you do not like the gym, you can still do most of it at home with lightweights, body weight or resistance bands.

The weight must be relatively heavy. Aim to do 6-8 reps. You are not looking to add another aerobic workout here. In the beginning there will be a little trial and error to see what weight you need to lift.

Start light and go up slowly.

Monitor if you have any soreness the next day. You do not want to be so sore from weights that you can't do your other training the next day. Do not lift to the point of failure. Aim to fit in 2 short sessions per week. It is about training smarter, not harder.

The Best Triathlon Specific Exercises

Look to do relevant multi joint exercises. For example, leg press is better than seated knee extension as you are moving your hip, knee and ankle. Knee extension only moves the knee and makes you more prone to injury.

Common triathletes' niggles you may have come across are "swimmer's shoulder", "runner's knee", and "cyclist's back pain". All these conditions can be fixed or prevented by correct strength training.

Here Are The Best Strength Exercises for Triathlon

1. Basic Squat

These should be done with your feet hip-width apart, your feet straight, a bar bell on your shoulders or dumb bells in each hand (In the beginning just body weight is fine too).

Bend at the hips, keep your back straight, look straight ahead and bend your knees to approximately 80 degrees.

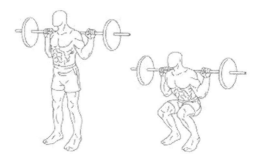

Push back up to the straight position. You should have no pain in your knees or your back.

You can do them at home without weights as well if you wish.

Make sure your knees do not collapse inwards.

Do 3 sets of 10 reps.

2. Leg Press

If you do go to the gym, a good alternative is the leg press.

Get someone to help you set yourself up correctly. Start light. Make sure your knees go straight over your feet and do not collapse inward. Push your knees straight, then let them come back to approximately 90 degrees.

Do 3 sets of 8 reps.

When you get good at this you can halve the weight and do single leg presses.

Good exercises include things that simulate your sport. Leg exercises should be predominantly one legged. Both running and cycling are sports done with one leg in front of the other.

Why would you train them together and not out in front of you?

3. One Leg Squat

I discussed this exercise in the running chapter. Stand on one leg. Use the wall for balance in the beginning, then work towards maintaining your balance yourself. Keep your back straight, bend your knee to 90 degrees, return to the straight position.

Do 3 sets of 20-30 reps.

Use body weight. Progress to dumb bells when you can.

Ditch leg curls and leg extensions. These are a waste of time, not functional and bad for your kneecaps.

Back strengthening

This is important for maintaining a good cycling position, especially up hills when pulling on the handlebars. It is good for maintaining an upright posture when running and good for swimming as well.

4. Seated row

Grab the bar or resistance band. Pull towards your chest, keeping elbows close to your body. Do not sway; keep your back still by using your core muscles. Return to start position. This exercise can also be performed with exercise bands.

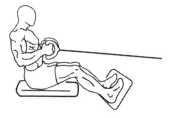

3 sets of 8 reps

Chin ups

Chin ups are an amazing exercise for shoulders and backs. They are great for swimming but also strengthen up your back for long hours on the bike. they help your overall posture.

Everyone should be able to lift their own body weight. However, a lot of people find this one hard. If you go to a gym, they usually have an assisted chin up machine. You can take off 20-40kgs and do assisted chin ups. As you get stronger, take more and more weight off until you are doing chin ups without help

Repeat 15 times, Do 3 sets.

Chest Strength Exercises

These are brilliant for strengthening shoulders for swimming.

Lie on your back, stabilizing it with your core muscles. Lift the bar (or dumb bells) up straight, and then lower yourself back to your chest. Do 3 sets of 10 reps.

You can also choose to lift kettle bells instead of a traditional bar for a good change.

Press-ups

The press-up is one of the best exercises ever invented! Even if you never go near a gym, do add this exercise to your routine. Great for shoulder stability, core stability, back stability. It costs nothing and you can do it anywhere. There is NO excuse for not doing this.

Go for stamina - 3 sets of 30 reps.

Calf strengthening

If you are prone to Achilles tendon problems or calf strains, add this in. Calf raises on the step.

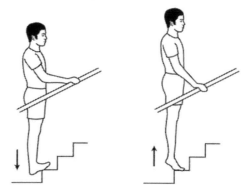

Do 3 x 15 reps, drop your heel below the horizontal, then push up all the way to your tiptoes.

If you go to a gym you can hold dumbbells. Some of them have machines where you can push up against resistance.

If you do calf strengthening at home with no added weights, make it more difficult after a few weeks by doing the calf raise with one leg.

Plank

And, of course, every time you do strength training, you will do your lovely core workouts, which are important in ALL the disciplines and will make massive differences to your race times.

The plank is one of the best.

Again, this requires NO equipment, costs nothing and there is no excuse for not doing it.

It is brilliant for maintaining your swim form, preventing back pain on the bike and ensuring you maintain good posture for your run.

Lie on the floor on your tummy. Prop yourself up on your elbows (or hands) and toes. Check that your back is straight.

Hold 3 x 2 minutes.

You can make this more difficult by raising one leg.

Also, add inside plank as well.

Of course, there are plenty more strength exercises you can do, and I am sure if you already go to the gym, you will know some of these.

Need more reasons to do strength training?

1. Improve your insulin sensitivity

    The pancreas secretes insulin in response to glucose in the blood stream. Endurance athletes require a ready supply of carbohydrates and glucose. Improving insulin sensitivity improves energy levels and supports a faster metabolism. If cells are insulin resistant you will have slower metabolism, poor performance and be at risk of developing diabetes. You will also see increased inflammation and accelerated ageing.

    Strength training is a well-known way to improve insulin sensitivity and manage diabetes.

2. Improve your reproductive health

    Endurance athletes have been shown to suffer reproductive health issues and impaired fertility from over training. Strength training improves hormone levels, fertility in both men and women and counteracts oxidative stress.

3. Strengthen your core

    Many studies show that dynamic strength training like squats and deadlifts massively improve core strength in functional ways for running and sports. Do not waste time doing hundreds of sit-ups. They are bad for your back and not a good functional exercise for triathlon.

4. Improve your anti oxidant levels

    Endurance training produces high levels of oxidative stress and chronic inflammation. Strength has been shown to counter this and improve anti oxidant levels.

5. Prevent injury

    Strength training helps correct structural muscle imbalances, preventing injuries like knee pain and shin splints. Strength work increases connective tissue strength and bone strength too.

6. Decrease body fat

    Strength training improves your body composition and the amount of calories you burn at rest. Strength training is the fastest way to burn more fat and if you have more lean muscle tissue and are lighter, your performances will be better.

7. Get faster

    Strength training improves your body's ability to use oxygen and energy. It will require less oxygen over time to achieve the same speed. Strength training improves resistance to fatigue and also improves firing in the fast twitch fibers.

This is so important that I will repeat it: strength training is essential if you are a triathlete, more important if you are over 35 years old, and even more important if you are trying to improve your performance without adding more hours to your training.

Strength training WILL make you faster and has so many benefits you would be crazy NOT to add it in to your weekly program.

The only instances where it has not shown a result are:

- The athlete lifted weights that were too light.
- The athlete gave up after 3-4 weeks. You will see a measurable result after 7-8 weeks.

Even if you do nothing else in this book but apply the exercises in this chapter, your triathlon performance will sky rocket. It is that important.

Chapter 7:

Grab The Nutritional Advantage

When I ask triathletes what their nutrition plan is, many of them are stumped and look at me blankly. Many athletes spend hours and hours perfecting their training schedule, their equipment and their clothing, leaving absolutely nothing to chance. But when it comes to their diet, they simply eat whatever they feel like.

They do not alter their diet much based on where they are in their training year or what their current goals are. It continues to amaze me.

Here I will give you the overview of nutrition, major factors to be aware of and also discuss nutrition periodization, which is an area that pays massive dividends but many athletes, including many elites, simply ignore.

What you eat plays a big role in how well you perform and how fast you recover from training sessions and from races. Of course, some triathletes kid themselves, thinking that they are not fat so they can eat what they like.

However, without the right fuel, you will not perform to your best, you will recover slower and you will feel more tired on a day-to-day basis than you will if you eat properly. Naturally you can have the odd treat on occasion but be careful to ensure the majority of your diet is from high-quality unprocessed food.

Some people live on caffeine, sugar and energy drinks. Whilst they do give you a temporary boost in the moment, they actually drain energy from you long term.

They destroy your adrenal glands, disrupt blood sugar and result in a huge energy crash after the high. These are not foods that improve energy levels long term.

Nutrition for athletes has three main roles:

- Maximize performance
- Sustain maximal performance
- Rapid recovery

There are also decisions about when to eat based on when you train. It depends on the distances you will cover as to how close to exercise you eat and whether you eat during exercise. Ideally, you will want to eat about 2 hours before you train. However, in the practical world where you have to go to work, it often means a quick banana in the morning, some water, then train, then off to work and re-fuel along the way.

It does require preparation. Have something prepared for straight after training so you do not have a window of no fuel. 45 minutes straight after training is the critical time period to refuel before you get depleted.

There are three sources of fuel for the body: carbohydrate, fat and protein. The primary fuel for energy is carbohydrate. Carbohydrate is burned more efficiently than fat or protein. Energy can be released from carbohydrate three times as fast as it can be from fat.

The body can store approximately 2 hours worth of easy-to-supply carbohydrate. Then the stores of glycogen stored in muscle and the liver run out. For longer events, therefore, you will need to top up your carbohydrate stores. A diet high in carbohydrate (about 60% of your daily intake) is important.

If you start to run low on carbohydrates you will experience "bonking", where your body runs out of useable energy. For this reason we need to take on carbohydrate before and during exercise.

Why athletes need to include fat in their diet

Many endurance athletes are obsessed with their weight. High power to weight ratio will result in superior performances. Any extra fat you have to carry around on the bike or the run will result in you expending more energy to move the same distance.

Many athletes notice a boost in race times when they shed a few pounds. However, do not over-do it. Cutting out fat can have a negative impact on performance and you certainly need to be cautious of losing "weight" rather than just losing "fat".

Make sure you do not lose muscle tissue. Correct nutrition for athletes is very important.

It is better to monitor body fat% rather than just weight (as weight includes muscle and water).

Here are the optimal body fat% of triathletes:

Men

20-29yrs 4-10%
30-39yrs 5-12%
40-49yrs 6-15%
50+yrs 8-17%

Women

20-29yrs 10-16%
30-39yrs 11-17%
40-49yrs 13-20%
50+yrs 14-22%

Healthy fats are an enormous source of energy, delivering nine calories of energy per gram as opposed to carbohydrates and protein delivering four calories per gram.

Fat also prevents the breakdown of muscle protein and promotes faster recovery after a workout. In addition fat plays an important role in normal bodily functions. Typically a triathlete should be eating 30-35% diet in fats. Eat from a wide range of fats, including red meat, dairy, nuts and oil.

Yes, you will be a better, faster athlete if you are leaner but do not go mad. If you are seriously looking to reduce body weight in the early days of training, you may reduce fat intake to 20% but no more.

Weight loss is best done slowly. Be realistic and do not go for gimmicks. Losing 1lb a week is sustainable and will allow you to keep training. Losing 10lbs a week is not realistic and can be dangerous.

Simply changing your diet to healthy whole foods and increasing your exercise levels will have you losing all the weight you want at a steady, gradual pace.

Train your body from the inside out. Eat a variety of natural foods and keep your fluids up all the time. Athletes who consume adequate calories and nutrients train better, recover quicker and are less susceptible to illness.

Food timings

Before training: top up your muscle glycogen by eating carbohydrate. Eat a bagel and a bowl of pasta one or two hours before training.

During exercise: to prevent depletion of carbohydrate stores, which result in fatigue and poor performance, consume carbohydrate-rich sports drinks (for events over one hour).

After exercise: consuming glycogen speeds up muscle repair by replenishing glycogen stores. There is a "carbohydrate window" of about 30-45 minutes after exercise. This is the most important time to replenish stores to get maximum recovery. Studies show this makes a massive difference in rapid recovery. Eat bagels, fruit, or energy bars.

What About Protein?

Protein is essential for every athlete and is vital in promoting muscle repair, building size and strength of the muscle fibers and increasing the number and function of mitochondria (helps you produce more energy).

Nothing is better than protein the way nature intended complete with essential amino acids, the correct proportion of fat and minerals already included. Chicken, beef, eggs, nuts and dairy contain more than enough protein for an athlete.

If you are going for muscle strength you certainly require adequate protein but not excessive protein. More is not better.

Normally speaking, 0.5g-0.75g protein per pound of body weight is what you need. If you are looking to gain muscle tissue you may push that up to 1g of protein per pound of body weight.

So if you are a 200 pound body builder you would get 200 grams through a couple of eggs at breakfast, 2 cans of tuna at lunch and a large chicken breast at night. (Triathletes would need far less than this!). Any extra protein drinks are a wasted expense and just adds extra calories.

The generally accepted practice is 3:1 or 4:1 ratio of carbohydrate to protein for recovery.

Carb-loading: Fact or Fiction?

The science of carb-loading has changed somewhat in recent years. It is not just about ploughing down plates of pasta. But done correctly it can make a huge difference in endurance events like triathlon.

As mentioned before, the body can store enough glycogen for about 90-120 minutes of exercise, so if you are doing sprint triathlon, you don't need to change your diet significantly. Just maintain a good, well-balanced, healthy diet and fuel your body properly on race day prior to your event.

However, for longer distances this science is important to stop you from hitting the "wall" and running out of energy.

Carb-loading used to involve a program starting the week before the race. It involved hard exercise combined with carbohydrate depletion for three days in the final week. The next 3 days would involve very little exercise and overloading the carbs prior to the big race.

The theory behind this was it would encourage the body to store more glycogen.

However, it did not really work. What happened is the athletes would become very tired due to the carbohydrate depletion and hard exercise and lose morale and focus. Then they found it hard to stuff themselves to the required level at the end, feeling bloated, heavy and sluggish.

So the recent advice is to keep to your normal diet and exercise routine (obviously you are in the taper phase anyway) and simply add more carbohydrate to your diet in the last 3 days.

In general, you need 5-7g of carbohydrate for every kg body weight. In this carb-loading phase go for 8-10g for kg of body weight.

To reach your carbohydrate target, eat little and often throughout the day rather than going for huge meals.

Remember the important distinction: it is not about eating MORE calories overall. It is about <u>increasing the proportion</u> of carbohydrate in your diet.

Most athletes eat slightly less overall during the last week before an event because they are tapering and do not have the huge energy expenditure they had in previous weeks.

Examples of high carbohydrate meals include:

- Grilled chicken and rice
- Wholemeal toast and peanut butter
- Large bowl of spaghetti
- Cereal and milk

And yes, still include some protein, which will give you an energy boost and slow the digestion of carbohydrate, releasing energy slowly – perfect for endurance events!

Carbs During The Race

In any race over 60 minutes, taking in carbohydrates in the form of bars, gels or drinks is a good idea to spare muscle glycogen. For events longer than 2-3 hours, you will need to take in carb/protein mixes as studies have shown they help athletes perform significantly better than carbohydrate only drinks or food.

Iron needs for triathletes

Triathletes depend on efficient delivery of oxygen to working muscles. Iron carries oxygen to your muscles. Iron deficiency is prevalent in endurance athletes. This causes fatigue, headaches, dizziness and poor immunity.

Over training, work, stress can all take their toll on triathletes who are busy trying hard to fit it all in. Fatigue and chronic tiredness can slowly creep in and you can begin to think it is "normal". Most of the iron in the body is incorporated into hemoglobin, which helps the blood protein deliver oxygen to organs, muscles and all cells, and removes carbon dioxide.

Iron is continually lost from the body and needs to be replaced by dietary intake. If dietary intake is inadequate iron stores can become depleted. This results in lethargy, fatigue, pale skin and poor sports performance.

Did you know that when you sweat, you lose iron with each droplet?

If you are looking to boost muscle or endurance, it will be an uphill battle without adequate iron intake.

Aim to eat at least 18mg/day.

Iron comes in 2 forms: heme and non-heme.

Heme iron is found in animal flesh (red meats, chicken and fish) and is easily absorbed.

Non-heme iron is found in plant forms and is not easily absorbed, so vegetarians must carefully plan their diet. Many breads and breakfast cereals have commercially fortified iron.

Iron rich foods:

- Lean meat 1-3mg
- Beans and lentils 3-4mg
- Fortified breakfast cereal 18mg
- Spinach 2-3mg

Consuming vitamin C with your meal enhances uptake of iron to your system.

Also, be careful with excess tea and coffee as the tannins can reduce iron uptake by up to 50%.

Excessive iron can be toxic, so do not over-do it.

If you eat an iron rich diet but still feel you may be low in iron or suffer chronic fatigue, see your doctor for a blood test to identify the cause of the problem.

Calcium

Calcium helps build strong bones and teeth. A diet too low in calcium can leave you with brittle bones and a predisposition to fractures. Make sure you are getting 1300mg per day. Good sources include yoghurt, milk, cheese, spinach and broccoli.

Eat Often

The key to good nutrition for athletes is to snack regularly throughout the day. Always have a healthy snack on hand like nuts, seeds, berries, low fat yoghurt, a bagel or piece of fruit. It will stop you from getting too hungry and reaching for rubbish food.

As an athlete, hunger strikes at any time. Prepare in advance, eat healthy, real food and leave the pies, sausage rolls and chocolate bars for the spectators!

Nutrition periodization

This refers to matching your dietary needs to your physical training. As your training moves from base training to more intense work, to tapering, your nutrition needs to change. Fuelling your body for triathlon is more difficult than fuelling a car.

With a car you fill it with the same stuff each time it is empty. With triathlon you are fuelling several different energy systems from a choice of 3 different foods groups: fat, carbohydrate and protein. You must control the proportions of fuel, the ratios of the ingredients and the timings.

No wonder so many get it wrong or find it so confusing they chose to ignore it altogether and just "wing it".

During base training you are laying down the groundwork of aerobic conditioning and building endurance, not doing top end speed or power. Workouts are typically long and intensity fairly low. In this phase you want to achieve your body composition goals for the season. So if you wish to lose some body fat, now if the time to do it. You can safely drop some carbs without compromising performance.

A good ratio is carbohydrate 60%, protein 13% and fat 27%.

During the build phase, you are doing longer and harder efforts and spending more time at lactate threshold. You will need more carbohydrate and less fat as a source of energy. As a working guideline use carbs 65%, fat 20% and protein 15%.

A lack of carbs here could mean you never reach the intensities you are aiming for.

Make sure you do not restrict your carbs going into a hill session or high intensity workout. If you can't make the required intensity, what is the point?

During the <u>racing and peak training phase</u>, you are doing high intensity training. Drop the fat content to 15%, increase the protein to 17% for muscle recovery and carbs to 68%.

A week or two before a race you will be **tapering** the work output to ensure you arrive at the start line feeling fresh and fully recovered. If you continue to eat the same amount of calories as you did during a heavy training week, you risk putting on the pounds just prior to the race. Be conscious to restrict your overall calories a bit in proportion to your work output.

During **recovery phase**, increase the protein to 25% and decrease the carbohydrates to 55% and fat to 20%.

You need to focus on muscle repair. You do not want to be putting on weight.

The Ten Essential Habits of Highly Successful Triathletes:

Listen to hunger signals. To stay lean all year-round, learn to eat when you are hungry but when you are full, STOP eating. There is no need to stuff yourself just because it is there!

Sit down for meals. As a busy athlete juggling three sports, it's easy to eat on the go all the time. Sit down to eat meals and switch off distractions to fully enjoy your food and be aware of exactly what (and how much) you are putting in your body.

Don't overestimate calories burned. Resist the temptation to have a huge blow out on junk calories just because you did a hard training session. If you did a great session, congratulate yourself. Reward yourself with proper fuel and enjoy the fact that you probably burnt some body fat you could do without. Do not immediately put it all back on!

Get organized. Shop with a list and a plan for the week. Resist impulse buys when you are hungry. Have a plan for meals and snacks throughout the day.

Eat (healthy) fats. Fat is satiating and essential for optimal health, functioning and energy. This means you should eat fatty foods such as salmon, nuts, olive oil and coconut oil.

Get decent sleep. Calorie consumption increases when you are tired. Getting a full night's sleep will keep you on track.

Cut the caffeine. It is a good idea to cut out (or drastically cut down) your caffeine intake in the week before your race. This will make you much more sensitive to it on race day, giving you a much needed boost of energy.

Don't skip meals to lose weight. Getting overly hungry will just raise cortisol (stress hormone) levels and make weight loss harder. Plus, you are more likely to eventually break down and binge on sugar. Slow and steady is the rule for lasting weight loss.

Get enough protein. Protein is one of the main differences of men and women's diets. In general more men tend to be obsessed with protein whereas many women are not bothered about it or think it is only for body builders.

Most women need more protein in their diet to maintain muscle mass and help curb hunger pangs. Protein helps to give you that full feeling that you have eaten enough.

Pay attention to adequate hydration. Poor hydration can appear in the form of hunger. When you feel hungry, consider if you are really thirsty instead.

The "drink 8 glasses of water a day" rule is for the general population. It does not consider the sweat rates of athletes, what climate you live in, whether you are sitting in air conditioning all day and all sorts of other demands you may have in your life.

Make sure you drink frequently throughout the day, alternating between plain water and low sugar electrolyte drinks. Your urine should not be dark or clear, but straw colored.

Summary:

- Don't allow a bad diet to let you down.
- Pre plan your meals each week so you are not tempted to grab a take away or hit the sweets because you have nothing left in the house and don't have time to go to the shops.
- Eat to win. Eat to recover. Eat for fuel. Keep your energy levels up.
- Keep hydrated – often the brain mistakes being thirsty for being hungry.

Chapter 8:

Easy Bike Maintenance

Many triathletes can change a tire but when it comes to maintaining their bike, most just rely on the bike shop services. This is fine most of the time but there are a few things you should do each week to quickly check it and ensure you are safe when riding and also to extend the lifespan of your beloved machine.

The bike leg takes up the majority of the time in your race. In training, the bike will take up the majority of your training week. It is important to understand your machine and be able to check it over properly once a week to ensure it is in good working order.

Often we do not make the effort to learn how to properly maintain our bikes until something goes wrong. (And this will always happen when the bike shop is closed!).

It is not difficult to learn and it will pay massive dividends both in training and racing. You do not have to become an expert in everything but you should be able to change a flat tire, replace brake pads and do general chain maintenance.

In a race situation, if you get a puncture, you will need to quickly and efficiently change your tire, so please learn this and practice it many times in training. You may not get help from spectators or you will get disqualified. You should aim to change your tire in less than 1 minute and be on your way.

Bike maintenance is important for your own safety as well. Imagine you are out in the middle of nowhere with a flat tire, unable to get back. Do you really want to rely on help from a passing stranger?

Please make sure you are self-reliant.

I will teach you how to change a tire later in the chapter.

Some bike shops run bike maintenance tutorials, which are really worthwhile. You will be spending a considerable amount of money on your bike. It is your responsibility to maintain it and ensure it is in good working order.

Never go for a training ride without a couple of spare inner tubes, repair kit, tire levers and a light bike pump. Chances are, if you do carry this stuff, you will never need them but we all know what happens the day you leave the house without them.

By the way, these days it is always a good idea to carry a cell phone for safety. Some longer rides can take you quite a way out of your area, so tell your family or a friend where you are going, how long you will be gone and when you are expected back. If possible, try to find some friends of a similar standard to cycle with.

It is more fun and much safer.

Before Every Ride:

- Pump up your tires (there will be a recommended pressure in psi on the side of the tire). Know what this is and re-inflate your tires to this each time you ride. Usually for racing bikes the recommended pressure is 100-120psi. This will help you go faster and will prevent punctures.

- Make sure you clean and lube your chain. Apply degreaser. Wipe off with a clean rag and go over the links with an old toothbrush. Pay attention to the cogs and cassette too. Dry it off then re-lubricate with a chain lubricant. While here check the chain for signs of wear or rust.

- Clean your bike. Wet, damp conditions will cause dirt and grit off the roads to collect on your bike easily. Salt will get into your bike if you are in a coastal area, so wipe it down regularly. This will add years to the life of your bike.

- Check for rattles and loose nuts and bolts.

- Regularly check the tread on the tires for signs of wear and tear.

- Check the seat post is on firmly and the handle bar stem is tight.

- Check the wheel spokes: if they are bent or damaged, get the bike shop to replace them.

- Check all the gears work and the chain is free from dirt, dryness and rust.
- Check the brake cables for over stretching and fraying. Also, check if the brake lever is fully engaged before the brake pad stops the bike, you may need to replace the brake pads.
- Brake pads: check for cracking. Brake pads should contact the rim directly and squarely

Essential Bike Tools to Carry:

- Pump
- Patch kit
- Cell phone (charged)
- Spare inner tubes
- Tire levers
- ID: medical information like blood group, allergies, emergency contact information tag or wristband (in case you get hit by a car or have a nasty fall)
- Some money
- Wear a helmet, ALWAYS!

Check you buy the right size spare inner tubes! This may seem obvious but I have been out with a group training when someone got a flat and very smugly brought out their spare tube only to discover they had the wrong size! They were slightly red-faced having to ask a fellow cyclist if they could borrow theirs.

The size is indicated on the side of the tire. If you get a flat, simply replace the tube and repair the flat when you are back home.

Warning: always carry two spare tubes and a patch repair kit. It is not unheard of to get two flats on the same ride. It is also possible to immediately get a flat on the new tube because it pinches the rim. Very disheartening!

When you take the old tube out, carefully check the wheel for debris, nails or glass. Try to identify what caused the puncture and make sure it is still not inside the wheel. Otherwise, as soon as you pump up the new tube, it will puncture immediately and you will be extremely angry with yourself.

If you are with other riders, this can be extremely embarrassing as they will be very keen to get cycling again and watching you start again might cause a few comments to fly.

When you are back at home, repair the puncture. Find the hole by inflating the tire, then feeling the air coming out against your face or hearing the hissing sound. You could also run a sponge of soapy water over the tire and the water will bubble at the point of the puncture.

Clean your chain and your bike when it needs it. This really depends on the conditions.

Bike Lingo

Bicycles come with their own language and terminology.

Here are a few common terms you should know:

Bottom bracket: the bearing assembly the crank set spins on

Crank set: the big mechanism ring that the pedals are attached to

Front and rear derailleur: the front and back cogs that moves the gears

Headset: where the handlebars attach to the frame

Cassette: the cluster of sprockets that attaches to the hub on the rear wheel

Serial number: can be found underneath the bottom bracket. Make a note of it as it identifies your bike for insurance purposes or theft.

What To Check Once A Month

Wheels: Make sure the wheels are properly fastened and aligned correctly.

Steering: Check for looseness and tighten where necessary.

Pedals: Check they spin freely and tighten if necessary.

Gears: Check they all work and move up and down smoothly (It is best to leave any gear repairs or adjustments to a mechanic).

Frame: Inspect the frame for any signs of damage.

Wear old clothes that you don't mind getting covered in grease. Have some old rags and an old toothbrush handy. Buy a chain cleaner and a degreaser from the bike shop. It is best to take the wheels off once a month and give them a proper clean.

How to Change a Tire

If you can confidently change a tire in less than 2 minutes, feel free to skip this section.

If you do not know or have not practiced for a while, time yourself, then come back to this section if you need to.

This is a very important skill to have as a cyclist and will make you self-sufficient on the road and race ready in an event.

1. Remove the wheel from the bike. Most bikes now have quick releases. So it is easy to remove the wheel. Where

people sometimes go wrong is they forget about the brake calipers. Gently use the lever to release the brake calipers, unscrew the bolt on the axis and remove the wheel.

2. Unscrew the valve and deflate the tire.

3. Place a lever under the edge of the tire and hook the other lever under around a spoke. Do the same thing a few inches away with another lever. You may need to do this one more time; then you should be able to put your fingers underneath the tire and remove the tube.

4. Pump up the flat tire quickly and examine it for glass or debris. Remove the offending object carefully. If you can't see anything, check on the tire itself and run your fingers (carefully) around the inside of the wheel, checking for debris. You will be extremely frustrated if you pump up a new inner tube only to have it puncture straight away as there was still glass left in there.

5. If it is clean inside, slightly pump up the inner tube so it has some structure. This will make it easier to insert into the tire. Start with the valve, then insert the tube carefully.

6. Alternative: you may choose to repair the tire or you may have gotten more than one flat and need to repair the tire. Mark the hole with chalk. Use sandpaper from the puncture repair kit to scuff around the area where the hole is to help secure the patch to the tube. Spread glue evenly over the hole and wait for the glue to dry until it feels tacky to touch. Place a patch over and apply pressure. Or

use glue-less patches.

7. Hopefully, you will not have to do this very often but it is good to know how to do it.

8. Now it is time to put the tire back on your bike. Make sure one side of the tire is back in place. Some tires have an arrow that tells you which side the tire should go on to ensure the tread is facing the right way. Check your tires well in advance to see if your tires are like this. You don't want to go through all this only to realize later and have to start from scratch. The arrow points in the direction the tire rolls when the wheel is on the bike.

So now you should have the tube in, and one side of the tire in. The tricky part is the other side of the tire. You should be able to do ¾ of the job with your fingers.

Once you get to the last few inches, keep trying with your fingers. Be patient, breathe and keep working it on. If you use tire levers, you may pinch the new tube and get another puncture so take extreme care.

CO2 cartridge

These are brilliant for speed of changing a tire. They inflate the tube almost instantly to the right pressure. The problem with hand pumps is they are exhausting to inflate and difficult to get the right pressure.

In a race you want to make it as easy as possible to not waste valuable energy. Even on a training ride, you will be grateful for them. Once you use them once, you will never go back to hand pumps.

Of course, do not carry CO2 cartridges on a race if you have never used them before. Practice beforehand so you are familiar with them.

There are two main parts: the nozzle and the inflator. The inflators have two options: with or without flow control.

With flow control you can stop/start the pressure as you wish. Without flow control means you have one shot to get it right.

I buy the one with flow control - it just makes sense.

The cartridges come in 3 sizes: 12g, 16g and 25g. The smaller ones fill tubes up to 90 psi, the larger ones to 120+ psi.

They also come threaded or non-threaded. Threaded cartridges have less chance of going wrong. You can buy everything in a kit to make sure they all match for purpose.

Now let's go through how to pump it up.

You need a bit of air in the tube to get it to fit correctly. If you don't have a pump or flow control cartridge you can actually blow the tire up a bit just by depressing the valve with your tongue and blowing it up with your mouth. It's true - try it. I doubt you could get it to 120 psi this way but you can get enough air in there to start it off.

If you don't have flow control, take the inflator and attach it to the tube valve first. Do not attach it to the cartridge first (unless you have flow control). This reduces the chances of things going very wrong.

With the nozzle on the valve, it is time to screw in the cartridge. It should screw in easily at first, then come to a slight halt. This means you are about to break the seal and release the CO_2 into the tube.

Once you do this it will inflate in about 1.5 seconds. Depending on whether you have racing wheels or not, you may need to add one more cartridge as riding with low-pressure increase the risk of punctures.

Clean everything up and take your litter with you. If you leave the discarded kit in a race you will get a penalty.

Practice several times. The whole procedure may take you 15 minutes the first time. But after a few goes, you should be doing it in 2-3 minutes.

Slide the wheel back onto the frame and tighten it, gradually checking the wheel is aligned evenly between the brake pads. Make sure the brake pads are back in their correct position and the brake levers are back in place.

Very important last step that no one tells you

When you get home, deflate the CO2 and re-inflate with regular air. CO2 dissipates through rubber and you will lose half your psi by the next day.

Also, repair the puncture and make sure you have at least two spare tubes ready to go out for your next ride.

How To Repair A Broken Chain

Along with a flat tire, this is probably the next common occurrence that happens to cyclists.

You will need a chain tool. They are on most multi tools. If not, you should get one.

Fixing a bike chain on the street is no harder than fixing a flat tire if you are prepared.

The most common way your chain breaks is by pedaling full force at the same moment that you are shifting your front derailleur. Try to ease up on the pedal force when changing the front derailleur to reduce the chance of this happening.

Each link of a chain is held together by a steel pin/peg. With the chain tool (or a hammer) you can push the pins in and out, allowing you to remove or attach links.

Fixing a broken chain amounts to removing the broken link and re-attaching the remaining ends. On bikes with derailleurs there's enough extra links that you can remove a couple without a problem.

On a single-speed bike you probably won't have enough slack in the chain to remove a link; you'll need to borrow some links from an old chain or else buy a new one.

Step 1

Flip your bike over so you can get to the chain more easily.

Step 2

Take a look at the two broken ends. One end (possibly both) is damaged and needs to be removed. You need to remove 2 segments of the chain at the damaged end. If you just remove 1 segment you can't re-attach it.

Step 3

Place the chain into the groove in the chain tool at the spot you want to disconnect. If you are replacing a worn but unbroken chain you'll do the same thing here.

Turn the screw on the chain tool to start pushing the pin out of the chain. Be careful to keep the pin on the chain tool lined up with the pin on the chain; sometimes they like to slip around a bit.

Don't push the pin all the way out! Only push it far enough so the chain comes apart. You need to leave the last bit of the pin in the chain so you can push it back in later.

Step 4

Now feed the chain back onto your sprockets. It helps a lot if you have a friend who can hold the two ends in position while you reattach them.

Use the chain tool to push the pin back in.

This is the trickiest part to keep the tool lined up with the pin.

Note: many new chains come with a special link that makes the first-time installation possible without pushing any pins in.

Once the pin is in, the link you just attached will be stiff. Work it back and forth until it loosens enough to bend around the gears.

Summary

It will take you just a few minutes to do a weekly maintenance.

Definitely practice changing a tire quickly, time yourself if you have not done it much before. Put it on your schedule to do once a month and get your time down. Bike maintenance is one of the skills that triathletes require in races that no one tells you about until it is too late.

Get to know your bike and all the moving bits. The more you can do yourself, the better your bike will perform. No one will look after your bike as well as you.

Chapter 9:

Mental Attitude

Mental toughness is an important skill you definitely need in triathlon, whether your event is a sprint or an Ironman.

You will need it to complete your training.

You will need it to train for 3 sports at once.

You will need it to manage your time effectively.

You will need it to balance your nutrition and sleep requirements.

You will need it to overcome any injuries you may pick up along the way.

You need to learn how to suffer and push through anyway. You need to be able to focus on the goal and getting it done no matter what obstacles life throws in your way. Don't worry — they will come!

As well as training your body for the event, you are training your mind.

You must practice perseverance everyday when you are out training in the bad weather, when you cycle further than you have ever gone before, when you are in pain or hungry or tired. You must practice not quitting during training and not quitting during an event.

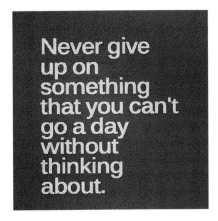

Never give up on something that you can't go a day without thinking about.

You must practice not quitting in the race when you are hurting and you see 10 athletes go past you looking comfortable. Dig deeper and see what you are really made of.

You Decide

Mental toughness is easy to get: you simply *decide* to have it.

You *decide* to get out and train when you don't feel 100 per cent. You *decide* not to quit during the race no matter how badly you feel and you *decide* to dig deeper and pass a few people at the end of a race.

It sounds easy but mental toughness alone isn't good enough. You need to combine that mental toughness with self-awareness and intelligence. You could decide to train hard every day and be tough enough to do it. However, after about 10 days you would be cooked and would have trouble finishing any race.

You need to know when to apply that mental toughness.

Most people go off very quickly at the start. As you are running your first half marathon, do you dig deeper and keep up with them? No, that would be stupidity. You need to have enough discipline and mental toughness to keep to your own race plan.

**Sometimes mental toughness is the ability
to hold back.**

Or if you have a shin injury that is getting worse, you might need to take the tough decision to pull out of a race before you develop full-blown shin splints.

Another scenario is you see someone on the bike and you spot him or her a couple of times on the run. You can tell you're at about the same level. Do you let that person beat you?

Not a chance!

Even though it is best to hold your own pace, you are still racing. Feel free to make friends on the race course but don't forget to compete with the people around you. In every race there are many smaller races going on.

Fitness, confidence, toughness, self-awareness, intelligence and, most importantly, discipline are what you need to be a successful endurance athlete. Everything has to come together. It's not easy for anyone.

The best mental approach to triathlon training and racing is to do as well as you can. Set your goals in advance. It might be to win a race, it might be to beat your time from last year, it might be just to finish!

When you achieve them, make sure you celebrate at the end.

Being nervous

Guess what? On race day everyone will be nervous, whether it is their first event or they are seasoned pros! Use that energy to give you power. To keep nerves under control, preparation is key.

You have done your physical training. Everyone is in the same boat. Do a pre-race warm-up to spin the legs and get in the zone. And remember to breathe.

Find some motivational sayings or a mantra you have prepared in advance that you can say to yourself over and over to help you focus on how good you are feeling, how strong you are, how much you are going to enjoy the race.

Get some family or friends to support you and give you encouragement.

Even during the race you may have to battle fragile mental or emotional states like boredom, fear, fatigue or self-doubt. Be prepared for this and banish these thoughts from your mind immediately. Fill your mind constantly with positive, strong thoughts and allow nothing else to enter your head.

Mental Rehearsal

Make sure along the way you do mental rehearsal and mental training.

This step is key to making sure you have run through the race many times before hand in your mind.

At least for 10 minutes, 3 times a week, sit down somewhere quiet and visualize race day. Visualize arriving at the venue and watching lots of people rushing around.

Visualize everything as vividly as you can,- the sights, the smells, the sounds.

Listen to the loudspeaker barking instructions, visualize yourself feeling confident and calm.

Visualize yourself arriving having everything you need. Watch yourself racking your bike and setting up your transition area.

Visualize yourself rehearsing the transition entrances and exits.

Visualize yourself having your last portion of fuel before zipping up your wetsuit - still feeling excited but calm and confident.

Visualize the gun going off and see yourself completing the perfect swim, an easy transition, cycling well, coming back in good time.

Visualize T2 going well, completing the run in a personal record and crossing the line to many cheers and applause, thrilled with your time and having had a fantastic race.

Tools for mental toughness

Here are 2 tools you can use:

Self Talk

An average person has 60,000 thoughts per day; most of them are negative! For example, "I'm hopeless at this sport", "Why am I bothering?" and so on.

"Extensive research in the sports psychology world confirms that an athlete's internal dialogue significantly influences performance."

Seltz 2009

It doesn't matter what happens in the race like a bad swim, or a puncture in the cycle. Simply focus on the present and what you can do well to improve things.

Often this negative self-talk is just a bad habit. You need to practice filling your mind up with positive thoughts. For example, celebrate every mile you have completed. Tell yourself you are enjoying it. Tell yourself you are looking forward to the bike, to the run.

You need to practice positive self talk in every training session so that on race day it comes naturally. Make it a new habit.

Plan to do nothing new on race day. If you don't do this in training and think that you will remember to do it in the race, let me tell you - you won't! There is too much going on and too much adrenaline and nerves, too many marshals and other people dashing about to start doing something new.

Visualization

I discussed earlier the power of visualization for race day.

Visualization is very important for every training session to help perfect your technique as quickly as possible.

This does not need to take long. Do it 2 minutes before you drift off to sleep. Do it while waiting at a red traffic light or waiting in a queue or for the kettle to boil.

See in your mind a perfect video of you swimming perfectly. For example, visualize your elbow coming out of the water, your fingertips entering the water in front of your shoulder. Visualize the strong pull through, your horizontal body position, your easy breathing manner and your powerful kick.

Visualize enjoying it, feeling strong and coming out of the water in the front of the pack.

Try to make it as real as possible. Feel the sun on your back and the water pressure as you pull through. Try to smell the chlorine or the sea salt. See yourself managing pressure and staying confident and in control. Picture the perfect stroke, the perfect cycle and the perfect run.

While you are doing your training, practice your perfect technique, and practice filling your mind with positive thoughts. Of course, training is tough most of the time, but try not to focus on the pain.

Instead, fill your mind with thoughts like:

"It's great to be out here in the fresh air."
"I'm getting stronger and stronger."
"I can't wait for the race."
"I am always confident and in control."
"The more it hurts, the better I get."

When any negative thought enters your head banish it immediately!

Pick one or two mantras that resonate with you and say them over and over with feeling to give you strength when you experience self-doubt or fatigue or feel like giving up.

That is the time to shout the mantra in your head and get back on track.

Practice these tools daily and you will find you approach the race with excitement instead of nerves and with eager anticipation instead of dread.

Goal Setting

You may be peaking for your big race of the year but make sure you set mini goals along the way. This keeps you on track; it also gives you mini celebrations along the way, which are really important. You are putting in a lot of time training and it is important that you observe that you are improving and achieving the whole way along not just on race day.

Make the goals specific and measurable.

For example, at the start of the year maybe you could run 5km in 29.38mins.

Your goal would NOT be simply "to get faster". It should be specific: "I will run 5km in 25 minutes by December 1st."

You might have a series of mini goals along the way to culminate in the race.

For example, if you had booked a half Ironman, maybe you could also book a couple of sprint distance triathlons, a couple of Olympic distance races and a 60-mile cycle sportive.

These will all give you race practice, packing your race bags, testing your nutrition and hydration and practicing your transitions.

Race experience is very valuable. If you are training for a triathlon, participating in swim only events or 5km/10km runs really helps with the whole racing experience. It also helps you to see what your body can do in a race. Often you will be surprised and produce results you never thought possible in training.

Summary

Many triathletes pay lip service to mental training. But very few actually schedule some practice. It is so important that most the pros from every sport hire a mind coach to help them truly engage the power of the brain. Anyone who does this wishes they started earlier.

If you actually do this a couple of times a week-you will reap fantastic rewards and your training will be more productive!

Chapter 10:

The 5 Most Common Triathlon Injuries and How to Treat Them

There is nothing worse than training hard all year, making sacrifices, missing friends' birthday parties, getting up at 5am to train before work, going to bed early, saying no to late night drinking sessions all with the thought of glory when you cross the finish line at the triathlon event of the year - only to get injured 3 weeks before hand and have to pull out.

This situation does happen to many athletes and it makes grown adults cry.

Most sports come with a risk of some injury. Thankfully, triathlon does not have the risks that come with boxing, rugby or other contact sports. Most of the injuries come from overuse (too much too soon) or biomechanical errors (poor technique).

This means they are avoidable.

These injuries account for over 80% of all triathlon injuries according to a sample of surveys conducted by universities in USA, UK and Australia. Other injuries in triathlon come from collisions with cars, collisions with other athletes and miscellaneous.

Running produces the highest number of injuries. It is a very technical sport with a lot of technique involved but most people never have one lesson or coaching session on "how to run". If you are like most people you go to the store, buy a pair of "good" running shoes and start running, and hope you were born with the running style of Usain Bolt.

Swimming tends to produce shoulder injuries and cycling tends to produce back or neck pain and sometimes knee pain.

One of the great things about triathlon is that it tends to be a balanced sport as you are training the whole body instead of simply pounding the pavements.

Triathletes can be an obsessive bunch though, so over use injuries are common; pushing through the pain and not bothering learning technique are major risk factors for getting injured.

Injuries are much easier to prevent than treat.

Often a couple of days off may prevent a niggle from becoming a full blown injury that may take 6 weeks to treat. So, follow your training program, schedule some rest days, listen to your body and avoid the injury in the first place!

Top 5 injuries

Here are the top 5 injuries, how to prevent them and how to treat them if they do appear.

Iliotibial (IT) Band Syndrome

This is the curse of runners across the globe.

You will generally feel pain on the outside of your knee. It comes on gradually. Initially, you think you can just run through it but then the pain gets worse until it completely debilitates you to the point that you are even limping when you walk. You may decide to have one or two days off. Finally, you can't feel it anymore.

Iliotibial Band Syndrome

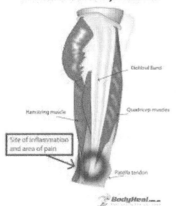

Great - you think it has gone. You start running again - all seems fine. But 10-15 minutes later, you can't believe it - the pain is still there!

After a few weeks of limiting your running, then trying to "run through the pain" and then resting and "hoping" it will just go away, you eventually must seek treatment and have 4-6 weeks off.

Sometimes cyclists will experience this too but the majority of sufferers are runners.

The IT band is a band of tissue that stretches from the hip to the knee down the outside of your leg. It gets aggravated by repetitive bending at the knee when you run, causing friction and inflammation at the knee joint.

It can flare up due to increasing mileage too quickly or due to poor running and cycling technique. Another major cause is weak gluteal muscles.

To successfully treat it:

- Rest from running or cycling.
- Get a sports massage on your IT band to loosen it off (or use a roller).
- Spend some time in the gym strengthening your gluteal muscles. Try exercises like squats, walking lunges and one-leg lunges, keeping your pelvis stable.
- If you get chronic IT band symptoms, buy a foam roller and roll on it every night after running to keep the IT band loose.
- Also, consider having a professional look at your gait and "how" you are running. Very often it is aggravated if your knee tends to drop in when you land. Go back and review the section on good running form if you suffer IT band issues.

Achilles Tendonitis

You will feel pain at your Achilles tendon. This is the tendon just above your heel bone. If you squeeze it, you will feel pain. It may look red or feel like there is a bump on it.

Sufferers describe extreme pain when they get out of bed in the morning; then it eases off as they get going and warm up. Sometimes it is very painful at the beginning of a run, then eases during the run.

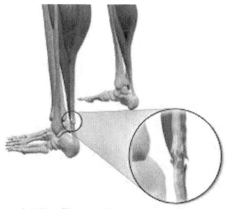

Achilles Tendon Tear

Do not ignore the pain, even if you can run through it. It will get worse! If it becomes chronic, you may have pain for 3-6 months or longer. If you leave it, you may be a risk of an Achilles tear.

This injury can occur due to increasing your mileage too soon, tight calf muscles, or poor technique (for example, over-pronation when your foot lands when running).

To treat it:

- Get a sports massage to loosen off the calf muscles and get some increased blood flow in the Achilles tendon.
- Stop running for a few weeks.
- Focus on calf stretches.
- Get a professional to look at your running technique and see if there are any improvements to be made.
- Strengthening the calf muscles can help – do one-legged calf raises 3 x 15 reps twice a day.

Patellar Tendonitis

You will feel pain in the center of your knee, almost right under the kneecap. You will feel it when cycling, running or walking up and down steps.

This usually happens due to tight quadriceps; the muscles the run down the front of your thigh. This pulls the kneecap against the thigh bone (femur).

It can also happen due to poor bike fit or poor cycling technique. Sometimes it happens simply due to increasing bike mileage too quickly.

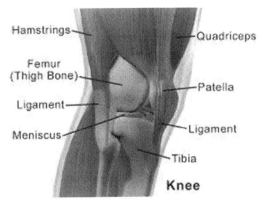

Knee

To treat it:

- If you have not had a bike fit done, book one.
- Stretch your quadriceps.
- Have a few weeks off the bike.
- Have someone cycle behind you and check if your knee is moving laterally or just pumping up and down.

Stress Fractures

You will feel pain in the bone during running; mainly it occurs in the shin. Sometimes you will feel it in the foot.

It usually occurs due to increasing your mileage too quickly. The constant pounding without sufficient rest produces tiny micro fractures in the bone.

To treat it:

- Rest from running at least 6-8 weeks.
- If it has not gone completely, get an x-ray or bone scan to confirm it but even then, the cure is more rest.

You do not have to stop training completely. You can do cycling, cross trainer, rowing machine, weights, swimming. Use the time to strengthen your weaknesses and make some gains in the other disciplines.

Review your program and see if there was a training error that led to this injury. Maybe you need an extra rest day, maybe you should do some flexibility work, maybe your core is weak and your running style is poor or maybe you pushed your mileage too quickly.

Do not be a hero and try to come back too quickly. You got the stress fracture from doing too much. So do not come back and repeat the same mistake. I know of people who have required a full year off running.

Listen to your body! Do not increase your mileage too quickly.

Rotator Cuff Tendonitis/Shoulder Pain

You notice a pain in your shoulder when your arm is extended above your head during the freestyle, front crawl stroke. It could feel like a dull pain or a sharp pain or a pinch.

This occurs due to muscle imbalance around the shoulder. Front crawl/freestyle develops the front of the shoulder and the chest muscles more than the back of the shoulder. It also occurs due to poor technique.

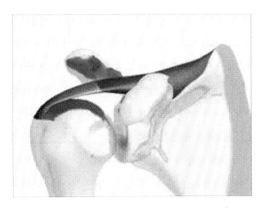

Do not build up to lots of mileage too quickly if you do not come from a swimming background or you do not have good swimming form.

Do make the time and the investment to take 10 lessons. Do the drills. Do the practice slowly at first, then follow up and get more feedback.

Some people try to take the cheap way out and buy a swim DVD or read a book on swim technique. This is certainly helpful but you need feedback from a qualified swim coach who can check your technique and make corrections. Whilst you may think you look like the next Michael Phelps, you most probably are very far from it.

Swimming is one of the most technical disciplines. In my view some lessons are imperative. From a racing point of view, good swim technique is important for gaining the quickest time with the most efficiency. Poor swimmers come out of the water completely exhausted because they have spent their time in the water thrashing about getting nowhere fast.

They have used so much energy they can barely get their wetsuit off and then they spend the first half of the bike leg recovering.

Fast swimming does not come from having big muscles, it comes from good technique.

To treat it:

- Stop swimming for a few weeks.
- Get some sports massages on the tight shoulder muscles.
- Stretch your chest and the front of your shoulder regularly.
- Book some lessons to look at your technique.
- Spend some time in the gym strengthening your posterior rotator cuff and rear deltoids. Use lightweights or resistance bands. Ask a personal trainer in the gym to check your technique during the exercises as well.
- When you return to the pool, start slowly and focus on your technique.

Most of these injuries are preventable. Remember good technique for all disciplines and build up mileage gradually. Also, notice how important strength training is to prevent injuries. Read the strength-training chapter again and implement it.

Signs of Overtraining

Too much mileage without enough recovery will not lead to niggles and serious injuries It will also result in decreased performance. You will become frustrated by training as hard as you can while noticing worse performances.

It takes many athletes years to learn that the body strengthens during recovery. During exercise, your body is under stress. Your body is suffering micro tears and trauma in the muscles and bones.

> **It is during rest and recovery that you get faster and stronger.**

These are the signs of overtraining:

- Disturbed sleep patterns disturbed (Consistent poor sleep will decrease levels of growth hormone - this is necessary to rebuild muscle fibers.)

- Lowered energy levels
- Bad moods, grouchy and irritable
- Poor appetite
- Poor immune system and frequent illness
- Unusually elevated resting heart rate

It does not just happen to Ironman athletes doing huge mileage. Recreational athletes suffer as well. We have to balance deadlines, work, chores, kids, bills. It does not take much to overload the system.

Remember, smart training will get you better results overall.

Chapter 11:

Your First Race

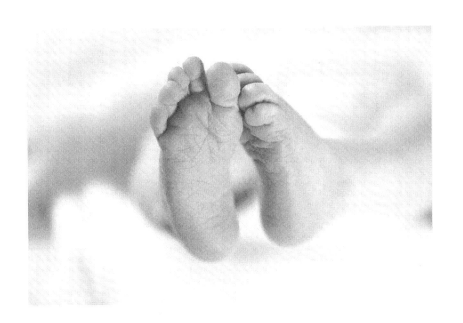

This information is invaluable in the week before your first race.

Even if you have raced before it may be a good refresher.

Try to make it as systematized as possible so you do the same thing every time.

Make a note of your routine in your training journal so you can refer to it later. Go back and review what worked and what did not work for you so you can adapt it later.

Taper

This is the week to really cut back on your training. You are not going to make any significant gains now. If you have not done adequate training you cannot cram it all into race week. You will only arrive at the start line exhausted and tired. Aim in the taper to allow your body to recover fully so you feel fresh and rested on the start line and can produce your best performance.

For sprint and Olympic distance, tapering the week before the race is sufficient.

If you are doing half Ironman or above, you will need to start your taper 2-3 weeks out.

For the purposes of this chapter, I will assume most of you will be doing sprint or Olympic distance. If you are doing longer race distances just adapt the distance and the timings a bit. The idea is to reduce the volume of training by 50% but not stop completely.

This is NOT a week to lay on the sofa every evening eating chips and burgers!

On Monday, Tuesday and Wednesday, do your normal warm up and some short, steady efforts that get you up to race speed. Take off all together on Thursday. The day before your race, do enough to bring you into a sweat for approximately 15-20 minutes.

You need to keep your motor neurons firing and your motor patterns active. Think about doing some race speed efforts and some drills. You do not want to feel sluggish and you are aiming to keep your body awake, fresh and on full alert.

Increase your visualization, picture the perfect race, picture your perfect form and say your mantras every day.

Use the rest of the time to get your kit together for the race and focus on your stretching; you'll also need great nutrition, lots of quality sleep, adequate hydration and positive visualization.

Picture yourself in the race doing very well, being in control and passing other competitors.

Sleep

Get as much sleep as you can. Sleep is essential for recovery and feeling as fresh and rested as you can. Most people do not sleep well the night before a race but make sure the rest of the week you sleep well or your race day performance will suffer (One night of poor sleep on the night before a race is fine and has been shown to make very little difference).

Nutrition

Do not skip meals the week before a race. Do not do any radical diets in an effort to shed weight. It will not help now but will only make you tired. Skip alcohol and reduce caffeine the week before as these dehydrate you, strip your body of vitamins and often interfere with sleep (Most athletes have greatly reduced their alcohol intake or given it up altogether).

Do not eat a large meal late at night before the race. Keep the meal simple with carbohydrates to top up your glycogen stores and minimal fat and fiber. Do not introduce anything new - stick to tried and tested simple meals that you know and love.

You may increase the proportion of carbohydrate in your diet but do not increase overall calories. You are doing less volume training overall so you do not want to be piling on the pounds.

The morning of the race try to eat 100-200g carbohydrate and plenty of fluids despite the nerves. Make sure your last meal is about 2-3 hours before the race. If you feel you need more, sip it in through your sports drink.

Again it is best to be low in fiber to minimize risk of an upset stomach. Try a bagel, banana, porridge or toast.

Take sports drinks, energy bars and gels with you and, depending on the length of your event, eat one of these before you start. If your race is 1.5hrs or less, you will only need water during the race.

If the race is longer than that, some extra calories will help you perform better. As a guide you will need to take in 250-500 calories per hour on the bike and slightly less than that on the run.

But individual needs vary and this depends on your intensity of racing, your body size and how used to ingesting food while exercising you are. You will have worked this out beforehand anyway. Do nothing new on race day.

Packing

A few days beforehand do a trial run pack. This is so you have enough time to get new supplies should you need to. Make sure you inspect everything. Are your goggles leaking? Are your tires pumped? Do you have spare tubes? Is your chain well-lubed and your bike serviced? Have you got your lucky socks ready? A change of clothes for the podium?

You should have prepared your checklist as you went along - review the chapter on transition. Go through the list I provided you and pack it. Make sure you know what bag you will take and that everything fits.

Check the transition points with the organizers beforehand. Some events have T1 and T2 in different points so you may need a T1 bag and T2 bag.

On Race Day

Get to the event early. Know where you are going. You will be stressed enough about the race without having to clock-watch, fight traffic and run from the car park to the start line stressed out of your brain.

There may be long queues of people registering. Make time to find a strategic spot for your bike as discussed earlier and make a mental note of where it is.

Wander around the expo if there is one and enjoy the atmosphere.

If there is a race briefing, attend it. There will be important reminders about the race, including rules about being disqualified, changes to the course or the conditions, which buoys you must swim around and all sorts of other information. Do not rely on following fellow competitors. It is possible that they are doing different distance races. Also, walk around the transition area.

Visualize and plan where you will exit the water, how you will run to your bike, where you will enter with the bike later and where you will run out. As I have already discussed, you will have practiced laying out your transition area several times and again the night before. So it should be completely automatic now. Lay it all out and do it again mentally to check you have everything and it is all in its right place.

Final set up checklist

- Rack and secure your bike.
- Place your towel on the ground parallel to your bike.
- Put your number on your race belt or pin it on your tri suit (personal preference).
- Make sure your running shoes are open and ready to go (with socks inside if you choose to use them).
- Make sure your cycling shoes are open and ready to go.

- Make sure you have a portion of towel free to stand on and wipe debris off your feet.
- Have a water bottle handy.
- Place your helmet on your bike with sunglasses inside.
- Reset your bike computer.
- Have the drink bottles you need filled up and on the bike. If you need gels or bars during the ride, make sure they are taped onto the bike already.
- Check your bike is in the right gear.
- Have your sun hat for running ready if you need one; have any extra nutrition you require (spare gels or sports drinks) handy.
- Have an after race snack ready to go that you can eat within 30 minutes of finishing. If you wait until you have chatted with supporters, watched (or participated in) the podium presentation, collected your gear, gone to the car and gone home or to the restaurant, it will be too late for a quick recovery, so prepare a snack you can eat straight away.

Warm Up

The purpose of a warm up is to get the blood flowing, the neural synapses firing, the body warm and the lungs breathing. This will be a big help with nerves on the day of the race. Stay warm in between your warm up and your race with a fleece or sweatshirt. It is a good idea to do 10-15 minutes of short bursts (jogging, cycling or swimming) short bursts with some quick drills in between.

Some gentle stretches are ok but do not do any deep, sustained stretches. This will slow you down. It is better to do dynamic stretches. Do things like knee raises, jumps and hops, skipping side to side, bum kicks. If you are allowed to jump in the water and swim 50-100 meters, do that (if it is not too cold).

Relax and breathe as much as possible. Visualize the race or listen to your favorite music that gets you pumped up and feeling like a champion. Chat to people if that relaxes you. Do not chat to anyone who may put a doubt in your mind.

Say your mantras and put positive winning messages in your head. Do NOT allow your brain to freak you out by the look of the other competitors or the other bikes.

Now is the time to practice confidence, positivity and control.

Only focus on what *you* can do.

Plenty of times I have been at races and thought the other competitors looked more fit, more trained or had a better bike than me. And plenty of times I have beaten all of them and they were nowhere to be seen! So do not get intimidated by looks. Keep visualizing your perfect race.

Chapter 12:

Putting It All Together Easily

Once you are through your first few races and getting into the sport, it may be worth joining a local club. This is a great place to meet like-minded people and get some great race tips and really good quality training. Also, many clubs race together and so you can have more fun and be part of a team. Most clubs cater for all levels of ability and ambitions.

Stock Take

It is a good habit to review your season at the end of each season. Write down what went really well and review your goals: did you achieve them, were they too ambitious, not ambitious enough?

What went really badly? Did you get injured? Did you go out for a spicy meal the night before the race and have a disaster? Did you get disqualified for any reason?

Try to draw as much learning as you can from your season. Then think about what you want to achieve next year.

How can you improve?

What changes can you make to your program? To your equipment?

Will you do more strength work or mental training?

Will you join a club or get a swim coach?

Will you try a new distance?

It is worth planning your next season and what your longer-term goals are. Maybe an Ironman 70.3 or the full Ironman distance? Whatever you decide to do, remember to have fun with it and enjoy yourself.

You will find it is a very friendly sport and you can do it all over the world. Get involved and have a blast and see what you are capable of!

What can go wrong?

There are five main reasons for failure in triathlon.

None the reasons listed below should not apply to you because you have read this book!

- Poor transitions
- Failure to practice at brick sessions (where you bike first then run straight away)
- Skipping workouts
- Poor nutrition
- Over training and burn out

These are all poor excuses for failure and show lack of planning and lack of doing what matters.

Remember training is the art of turning your weaknesses into strengths.

Training successfully is practicing the things in your precious spare time that will make the most difference to your event.

If you are already a great cyclist, you will probably not get a whole lot more out of going on another three-hour steady state ride. You will make up massive time by practicing a brick session and doing a one-hour cycle plus an immediate 30-minute run.

Remember, if your time is limited, think about each week in advance. Plan out what you must do, what you must achieve this week and add in what will make the biggest difference. Of course, if you are training for the Ironman, you will need to devote a LOT of time to training. However, if you are doing sprint or Olympic distance you can get away with training 5-10 hours a week. Just focus on training smart.

Try to keep some training kit with you in your car or office in case an opportunity arises. For example, a client cancels a meeting and you have a two-hour gap in your day. You could go for a one-hour run, have a quick shower, some lunch and be back in the office, refreshed and energized.

If you have to take little Johnny to the pool, use the time to do a 30-minute swim session yourself. You will still have time to see his last few laps where he turns and waves at you and you will feel great.

If you are going to meet your colleagues after work at 7.30pm for a few drinks on Friday after work, tell them you will be there at 8.30pm. Go to the gym. Do a 30-minute strength session and meet them afterwards. No one will mind and most will be envious of your discipline.

Just remember to make time for yourself and do not let another year pass where you do not achieve something for yourself, something you are really proud of!

There are different stages of training. We cannot train hard all the time but we should not do long, slow plods all the time either. The trick is to keep mixing it up and challenging your body. The skill is learning how to peak at the right time for your race.

Five Main Stages Of Training

Base Training

Many beginner triathletes go wrong right here at the start. They do not have the patience to do base training. This is the longer, slower training that some people see as slightly dull!

A training program will be effective only if it suits your ability, time commitments and goals. You need to see steady progress and achieve mini-goals along the way to keep motivation high. The aim is to build your aerobic capacity. This is one of the biggest factors in triathlon that will affect your racing. Without a good foundation, you will break down, burn out or get injured later in the season.

For 12 weeks or so you will work in the aerobic zone, teaching your body to burn fat instead of sugar for fuel. This is lower intensity. So either train at a level you feel comfortable without being breathless or strap a heart rate monitor on; these are very cheap these days. After you build your base, you can focus on adding speed and power and training at anaerobic levels.

To calculate your aerobic heart rate zone:

Take 180 minus your age. If you do not train and are unfit, take 5 beats from this number. If you already train 5-7 times a week, add 5 beats to this number.

This number is your upper limit. In this phase you are not training to the point of burning muscles. You are teaching your body to burn fat. You may feel this is very easy without much perceived effort. This is correct – keep going!

For the first 12 weeks of the season, you should not go above this heart rate. Try to keep within 80% of it. So if your maximum heart rate is 150bpm, try to stay 120-150bpm for 12 weeks. Walk up the hills if you have to, put the bike in a small chain ring. Do not cheat!

Build Phase

In the build phase you have built your aerobic engine. You now focus on switching on and developing the fast twitch fibers in your muscles. You will be adding speed work and increasing the intensity and volume of your training. You will still be including some lower intensity sessions each week as easy recovery workouts and to maintain your aerobic base.

Interval training will increase your speed, strength, lactic acid threshold and fast twitch fibers. Each speed session should have about 15-25 minutes of high heart rate work in it.

So you may be doing 8 x 1000 meters running or 7 x 2 minutes on the bike; 3 x 1minutes sprints.

Doing 5-10 minutes is not enough; doing 30-35 minutes is too much.

As a general rule you should be doing 2 sessions per week of this. Train on the bike one day and run and swim the other day.

Please note that each one takes 2-3 days to recover from. Apply gradual increases in intensity. This is the phase where you are at high risk of injury. Continue to listen to your body.

Start to ease off the weights room now and focus more on sports-specific strength. For example, use hill running and hill repeats on the bike as your resistance work, so it is specific to your sport.

When you do speed work, your body releases hormones, which build new muscle tissue. However, if you do too many weeks in a row of hard, high intensity work, your muscles will start to break down. So keep checking your training diary and monitor your performances.

Start the first one at an easy pace then build the pace with each interval. If at the end you feel your form and technique slipping, ease off the speed again as you do not want to practice bad habits. Keep good form at all times.

Lactate Threshold

You may have heard of "training at your lactate threshold".

Lactic Acid Threshold (LT) is the highest intensity at which the body can recycle lactic acid as quickly as it is produced. Lactic acid is the waste product muscle produces when it is working. It is the substance that causes working muscles to burn during exercise. At this intensity, you are working very hard, but can still maintain exercise because lactic acid levels in the blood and muscles are steady, not increasing. The body can still get rid of the lactic acid fast enough.

However, pushing your body beyond this threshold causes lactic acid to build up and creates premature fatigue and delayed recovery. This is that familiar feeling of burning in your muscles, rubbery legs and rapid breathing when you are really pushing hard. If you can train just below lactate threshold you will be teaching your body to produce less lactic acid and remove it faster. You will be able to produce more force without fatigue.

The most accurate way to find your lactate threshold is in the lab with blood tests. However, given that most readers of this book will not be Olympic athletes with access to labs and technicians, you can do it yourself. Simply monitor your heart rate as you exercise with a heart rate monitor. Notice the point at which your breathing changes and your legs start to burn. Observe this on a few runs and bike rides. It will be around the same place.

The other way to do it is in running. Warm up for 10 minutes, then run a 30-minute time trial. Your average heart rate for the last 20 minutes is your lactate threshold.

If you train below this most of the time you will be able to continue for longer.

Most competitors use this in racing as well to make sure they do not "blow up" during the race and are unable to continue.

Peak Phase

In the peak phase you aim to consolidate the fitness and performance gains you have made. In this phase you reduce your workload volume but the intensity is maintained or increased. You may be looking at things like maintaining power output for a defined period.

This is where you start to understand what your race pace is. This time can be as long as 8 weeks so during these 4-8 weeks you can do some time trials at race pace to see how you handle the speed, intensity and work out the fuel you will need during a race.

It may be that you use a particular drink on the bike during lower intensity but when you increase the pace it may not agree with you and you may need to change. This is the time also to train at race pace. Wear your race kit.

Set up your bike for racing and your trainers for running with the race laces.

During this phase you will feel more fatigued and tired. That is fine; you are not racing yet. Get plenty of sleep and eat well. Not every session is intense. Mix it up and make sure you are not wrecked for the next couple of days. The trick is to train hard enough so you can keep training but to make good gains based on your base phase.

The better the base you have, the better your intensity will be. The saying is – the broader the base the higher the peak!

I split my training into 4-week blocks during this phase. Week 1 and 2 are less mileage often at a higher pace/ heart rate/ power, with the same number of sessions just building up some muscle endurance slowly. Week 3 contains less hours and less sessions but for each discipline do a race pace session so maybe a 1k swim at race pace (or 400m if you are doing sprints), a 10 mile bike time trial and maybe a 5 or 10k run at race pace. Do shorter distances than your race and don't go faster than you would in a race. Week 4 is then back to longer sessions with hill repeats and more intensity.

If it is an 8 week block then repeat weeks 1 to 4 but slightly faster and with more muscle endurance. During this time you will do more brick sessions and you should be using your race bike if you have one.

In this block it would be great if you could do a shorter race for practice.

Don't worry about the times. Just do it for the experience of managing stress, transitions, race nutrition and putting it all together. You will gain a lot of knowledge by doing this.

Racing Phase

In this phase you are participating in races. You are ready. You are using maximum effort in the race. Depending on the distance, you will taper for a certain period of time before the race. As we discussed earlier, tapering is backing off training and getting ready to race.

This phase could well last for months as you may be doing multiple races in a season.

If so, keep the intensity high and make sure you recover properly after a big race.

Set races out in order of importance and label them A, B and C races. Plan your race schedule around your A race and work towards it. If it is a B or C race, do not worry about the time. Just enjoy it. Use the experience and get better. If there is a big gap between races, go back and do a little base. Then build like before, only on shorter timescales to keep your fitness up.

Recovery Phase

The other aspect of training that is rarely mentioned is recovery!

Recovery is where your body adapts to the stress placed on it from exercise, your energy systems develop and your muscles grow. Build into your program at least one day off per week during training.

If you are starting from scratch, build in at least two days off per week.

As you move from your build phase into your speed work, start doing some higher intensity. Build in easier training weeks where you may do 60% the training volume of the previous weeks. This will prevent burn out and injury.

Training Zones

If you have been around training and sports for a while you will probably have come across training zones. These are heart rate zones that you work at during different stages in your training. I have provided you a sample 6-week plan as an example for you to play with.

This is not to follow to the letter. Use it as a guideline. Everyone will be at different levels of fitness and have different experience levels.

This plan is a sample for someone already averagely fit who wants to do a sprint triathlon in 6 weeks. (Remember, it is not the only way to train. It is just an example.)

You'll work out about 3 hours per week in the first two weeks, close to 5 hours in weeks three and four, 5 hours and 45 minutes in the fifth week, and just 1 hour and 45 minutes leading up to your race. Each intensity level, or training "zone," corresponds to a specific target heart rate in relation to your maximum heart rate (sometimes calculated as 220 minus your age).

Zone I: Training Zone I workouts should be performed at 50-60% of maximum heart rate. This should feel easy. Your breathing should be slightly elevated, but you should be able to hold a conversation without trouble.

Zone II: Training Zone II workouts should be performed at 60-70% of maximum heart rate. This is a moderately easy pace. Your breathing will feel more labored, but you should still be able to talk.

Zone III: Training Zone III workouts should be performed at 70-80% of maximum heart rate. This is a moderate pace. It'll be hard to hold a conversation—you can spit out a few words at a time.

Zone IV: Training Zone IV workouts should be performed at 80-90% of maximum heart rate. This is a moderately hard pace. You'll be struggling to talk. But remember that it's not all out. You should still be able to maintain this pace for around 20-40 minutes.

Example Training Plan

For your reference, here is an example of a beginner's training plan for a sprint triathlon. It is only for reference and will not be suitable for many of you. But if you have never done anything like this before, it will give you a general idea of how to structure a training plan.

Obviously, as I pointed out before, your base training might be twelve weeks by itself, especially if you are doing a longer triathlon. So please adapt it to your existing fitness level, your goals, your planned races timings and your planned race distances.

This plan is a six week plan for a sprint triathlon.

Week 1

Monday: Rest
Tuesday: Swim for 30 minutes in Zone I
Wednesday: Run for 40 minutes in Zone I; strength train for 20 minutes
Thursday: Rest
Friday: Rest
Saturday: Bike for 60 minutes in Zone I; strength train for 20 minutes
Sunday: Swim for 15 minutes in Zone I

Week 2

Monday: Rest
Tuesday: Swim for 30 minutes in Zone II
Wednesday: Run for 40 minutes in Zone II; strength train for 20 minutes
Thursday: Rest
Friday: Rest
Saturday: Bike for 60 minutes in Zone II; strength train for 20 minutes
Sunday: Swim for 15 minutes in Zone I

Week 3

Monday: Rest
Tuesday: Swim for 30 minutes in Zone II

Wednesday: Run for 30 minutes in Zone III; strength train for 40 minutes

Thursday: Swim for 30 minutes in Zone I; bike for 60 minutes in Zone III

Friday: Rest

Saturday: Brick workout: Bike for 50 minutes in Zone I and run for 20 minutes in Zone II

Sunday: Strength train for 20 minutes

Week 4

Monday: Rest

Tuesday: Swim for 30 minutes in Zone II

Wednesday: Run for 40 minutes in Zone II; strength train for 40 minutes

Thursday: Swim for 40 minutes in Zone II; bike for 60 minutes in Zone III

Friday: Rest

Saturday: Brick workout: Bike for 50 minutes in Zone I and run for 20 minutes in Zone II

Sunday: Strength train for 20 minutes

Week 5

Monday: Rest

Tuesday: Swim for 40 minutes in Zone III

Wednesday: Bike for 30 minutes in Zone I; run for 45 minutes in Zone II; strength train for 40 minutes

Thursday: Bike for 60 minutes in Zone II

Friday: Rest

Saturday: Brick workout/test triathlon: Swim for 30 minutes in Zone I, bike for 50 minutes in Zone II, and run for 30 minutes in Zone I

Sunday: Strength train for 20 minutes

Week 6

Monday: Rest
Tuesday: Bike for 40 minutes in Zone I
Wednesday: Swim for 25 minutes in Zone I
Thursday: Run for 20 minutes in Zone I
Friday: Rest
Saturday: Swim for 15 minutes in Zone I; bike for 15 minutes in Zone I
Sunday: Race day

Taper

The taper is one of the mysteries of an athlete. In theory it sounds brilliant. Great, a whole week off training before my event, excellent!

In practice it is very hard to do as you have put in so much work, so much training and you feel like it is all going to waste. You imagine all your competitors are still out there doing some extra hill sessions.

However, you cannot cheat a taper. In the week before a race you need to allow your muscles to re-fuel and feel fresh and you should be gagging to get out there at the start line.

Also, when you do this you will notice you feel sluggish, lethargic and tired. This is NORMAL! Allow yourself to repair from hard training weeks guilt free.

How long to taper for varies according to the race you are preparing for. In general, for a sprint distance allow one week, for an Olympic distance allow 10 days, for a half Ironman allow 2 weeks, for an Ironman allow 4 weeks.

This does not mean you stop everything for 4 weeks. It means gradually reducing volume and intensity of training.

It also means not filling every spare minute with other stuff you may have neglected during your training. Rest means rest.

Use the time to focus on your positive visualization, your flexibility and your technique. Do easy sessions. Make sure you are hydrated and eating well. Enjoy!

Off Season

What should I do in the off-season?

Some people do nothing, get out of shape, put on weight and lose all the benefits they gained during the year. Getting back to race fitness is such a hard slog again, this is not recommended.

You certainly do need a break. Do all the things you love to do. Do unstructured sport. Go skiing. Play with the kids. Try rollerblading. Try new activities. Meet up with old friends. Have fun!

The off-season is a great time to work on your weaknesses. For example, if your run was hampered this year with ongoing Achilles problems and calf tears, go and see a sports physiotherapist or a running coach to look at your running technique. Look at your muscle flexibility and strength and address this problem now. Do not ignore it or wait until next season starts and go through all the agony of dealing with ongoing injuries and missing training again.

If your bike is uncomfortable, get a specialized bike fit assessment done or buy a new one.

It is important in triathlon to peak at the right times. If you go off and train really hard in the winter and impress everyone with your January times, it is likely that you will be burnt out by the summer and miss races through injury. Certainly keep your fitness up but do have some time off. Work on your flexibility and your core muscles. The off-season is also a good time to work on your all-body strength as well. Get to the gym and make sure you are stronger next year than this year.

Chrissie Wellington (four time World Ironman Champion) speaks of the joy of "stripping down" on her blog. This does not mean naked training! But it does mean training for the pure fun of it — without analyzing heart rates, power outputs, split times and the weight of her water bottles. She said the joy of just running or cycling without all the gadgets is fantastic after a season.

In fact, she recalls with her first race:

When I did my first ironman in 2007, I borrowed my team mate's tri shorts...I didn't have a swim skin – I simply wore my swimsuit over the top of my race kit, I had training wheels, I asked an age group athlete friend about nutrition and she lent me some of her drink. And before Kona six weeks later... my pedal broke and I fixed it with industrial glue, I stayed in a two bed apartment up a 20% degree slope which I biked up every day with my shopping on my back, sleeping on a single bed that was like a trampoline, sharing a room with a Spanish guy I had never met. I hadn't had a bike fit, my sunglasses were £20 from a petrol station, I got about 2 hours shut eye the night before the race because the next door neighbors were having a full volume, ear blasting depriving domestic. And I won.

Inspirational! So do not worry if you do not have all the best gear, all the sports science manuals, all the charts and graphs at your fingertips. Simply do what needs to be done – and that is train!

Start training now, then come back and start your training journal straight away. Re-focus on your goals and the races you have planned this season and remember to enjoy it! Have fun and be proud of yourself!

Handy Race Day Check List

Swim

- Swim cap
- Ear plugs
- Swimming suit or tri suit
- Wetsuit
- Goggles
- Spare goggles

Bike

- Water bottles
- Bike
- Helmet
- Bike shoes (socks)
- Nutrition
- Pump
- Tire Levers
- Co2 cartridge (if necessary)
- Spare inner tubes
- Tire repair kit
- Sunglasses
- Sunscreen
- Cycling shirt, cycling shorts (or trisuit)
- Floor bike pump (before the race to get tires in perfect condition to prevent punctures and for maximum race speed)

Run

- Fuel belt
- Hat
- Running shoes
- Socks (if you choose to have them)
- Water bottle
- Towel
- Orthotics
- Sports bra

Other Essentials You Might Not Have Thought Of

Ask the organizers about whether there are lockers to leave your car keys, money, cell phone if you are going to the race solo. Of course, if you have friends and family, they will come in very useful for this purpose.

Other useful items you will need:

- Large plastic bags
- Small towel
- Beach towel
- Chamois
- Full change of clothes, including warm gear
- Deodorant
- Baby wipes to wipe down (if there is no shower)
- Shampoo/conditioner/shower gel (if there is a shower)
- Money for post race massage, snacks or photos
- Extra hair ties
- Pair of flip flops or extra shoes
- Post race snacks – chocolate, snack bars, energy drink of choice, bananas, nuts
- Lipstick (for podium photos!!)

- Camera
- Race tickets
- Hotel Tickets
- Airline tickets
- Passport/ID if necessary
- Directions to the hotel/to the race
- Chain lube
- Toilet paper
- Head light (if doing Ironman!)
- Heart rate monitor
- Wrist watch

The Rules Of Racing

You do not want to do all that training, discipline and strict nutrition to get disqualified during the race.

There is a densely worded race rules booklet, which is 25-30 pages long, depending on the version you get, which you are free to read and digest if you want. However, I suggest you spend the time training and skim through this summary I have prepared for you.

These rules are very similar in most jurisdictions.

Don't litter

You will be taking on drinks, gels and protein bars during the race depending on your distance. If you are seen throwing the empty packets on the street, you will incur a time penalty. If you can't reach the pocket in your shirt, simply tuck it up under your Lycra shorts leg. No problem. Do not suffer unnecessary time penalties. This is just foolish.

No IPod

For safety's sake, no music is allowed to be blasting in your ears. If you prefer music when you train, make sure you do a few weeks towards the end of your training prior to the race without music to get used to the silence.

Focus on your body, your breathing and positive affirmations as you get closer and closer to the finish line with every step and every pedal stroke. A good motto to remember is "do nothing new on race day".

No external assistance

Whilst your family and friends can be there cheering you on from the sidelines, they cannot give you any advantage. They cannot hand you a drink bottle, a sun hat or anything else.

The race must be completed by yourself.

Keep your own pace

Your family, friends or coach cannot shout your time from the sidelines or run alongside you to pace you or give you any help whatsoever. Make sure they understand this. You do not want to be disqualified because someone thought they would try to be "helpful".

Swim around the buoy

This is very important. Sometimes the race can seem like a washing machine. Adrenaline is high and everyone is converging on the same spot, trying to take the quickest line. Whatever happens, do not cut the corner. You MUST swim around the buoy.

Do not cycle in the transition area

Once you grab your bike after the swim, you will be focused on getting on your bike as soon as possible. Do not be tempted to jump too early. You must pass the mount line. Jonathan Brownlee received a penalty in the Olympics for doing this and it probably cost him a silver medal.

When you come back to T2, you must get off your bike at the dismount line and walk or jog your bike to the rack. Do not attempt to ride your bike to your rack.

Buckle your helmet

Officials are very strict on this one. You cannot even be fiddling with your strap as you mount your bike. My advice is to put your helmet on and buckle it properly before you even touch your bike or it could be instant disqualification.

You must keep your helmet on until the bike has been racked. Do not take it off when you dismount.

No drafting

Drafting behind a fellow cyclist means you work 30% less. The rule is 1 meter to the left and right and 7 meters behind is the zone. Once you are in this zone you have 15 seconds to pass or you will be in trouble. 7 meters is equal to 3 bike lengths. Drafting is a huge advantage and not allowed in most races (There are some draft legal races; make sure you know the rules for your race).

Stay on the course

Make sure you read the course directions before the race. Also, pay attention to race signs and the marshals when on the bike and run legs. Do not cut any corners or come off the path.

Training Principles Summary

Congratulations for reading this far!

You definitely have the discipline and dedication to make it as a triathlete.

We have gone through a huge amount of information. There is a lot to absorb and take in.

Here is a brief summary of the major points:

Do not get caught up in the details. You can return to each chapter as they become relevant. It will mean different things to you at different stages of your training.

You have a good overview now and will already know more about triathlon than the majority of people in their first season, so remember:

- Make every session count.
- Include enough rest – listen to your body.
- Have an easy training week once a month.
- Mix up your training sessions between short, hard, long and slow.

Training improves so many different component parts:

- Cardiovascular system: efficient delivery of oxygen to the muscles and a stronger heart
- Increased supply of blood vessels and mitochondria (energy cells) to the muscles,
- Stronger joints, ligaments and bones
- Improved running technique
- Improved metabolic system (Your body becomes better able to convert fat, carbohydrate and protein to energy.)
- Improved body composition - less fat, more muscle

Be Yourself, Find Yourself and Be True to Yourself

Remember to nurture yourself first and you will have more vitality and energy to give to others. You CAN do this and still have enough time for your family, work and social life.

Triathlon has overtaken marathon as the new challenge! You will get amazing bragging rights, develop a lean, toned body, find a whole new gang of friends, gain incredible self confidence and thoroughly enjoy the whole process.

Stand up and be a powerful example to your children, your partner and your work colleagues. Grow into a stronger person, a goal achiever, one who overcomes obstacles and does what others merely talk about. Live with purpose and with action.

Practice your training on a daily basis.

It is what you do each and every day that counts.

Not just the show time at a race. It is the getting up 40 minutes early to cycle before work. It is the going for a jog even though it is raining. It is the stretching for 15 minutes when you get in from a run. It is the discipline to say "no" to your 10km run written in your program because you feel a "tweak" in your calf.

It is the sum of all these things that will determine who you are as an athlete.

Are you full of excuses "why not?" "I pulled out of the race because..."

Or

Are you full of results and achievements, bursting with pride when you ring up your mum or dad to share it with them or when you see your kids and partner at the finish line cheering you in?

It is building a team of support all around you, all pulling in the same direction to help you become a better person, a better athlete and an all-round winner.

So jump right in and enjoy the tremendous journey that awaits you.

***

I am so excited for you and can't wait to hear your stories and results.

Please contact me at dan@triathlon-hacks.co.uk

If you enjoyed the book, would you please spare a minute and write a review?

It makes a huge big difference and I would really appreciate it

Stay updated and continue to receive the latest information and incredible training tips

http://www.triathlon-hacks.com
https://twitter.com/sam_triathlon
https://www.facebook.com

Click here to get your **free download** on how I took 17% off my triathlon race performance by training less!

***

About the author:

Dan Golding

I discovered the triathlon world in 2005.

It is fair to say I became slightly obsessed! This has probably happened to many of you. We triathletes tend to be an obsessive bunch. I love it- hey- there are worse things I could be obsessed about.

Triathlon has been a massive force for good in my life and given me structure, superb fitness, a bunch of cool friends who kick my ass and a lot of travel opportunities. My favourite distance is Olympic and 70.3. I am planning Ironman in 2017.

Triathlon has taught me some important lessons:

- **To never give up no matter how hopeless it seems right now**
- **Pain is temporary, results last forever**
- **To set unrealistic goals and work through every obstacle to make it happen no matter what**
- **That no matter how rubbish you feel right now, things will get better-eventually**
- **No matter how much you prepare, things sometimes still go wrong- Keep a sense of humour**

And much more- I mean the lessons keep coming right?

So what do I do now?

I have written a best selling book, I am half way through my next book on 70.3 (let me know if you want to go on the wait list for pre-launch).

I am also fortunate to have been invited to write with the excellent team at Triathlon Hacks, I coach clients 1:1 and online and I still swim, bike, run. I think this is in my blood now- I don't know that I will ever stop, though I certainly train smarter now and have added a lot of gym strength work, yoga and I am diligent with my nutrition.

* I travel a lot and currently live in Asia

* I love surfing- this feeds my soul and is my meditation

* I love House of Cards and James Bond movies (I keep waiting for the call up to be the next Bond)

* Family is super important to me- I have one gorgeous son name Toby- he is now 3 years old (and of course has his first bike-though my wife won't let me get him an aero helmet :)).

* I am the best cook in our household- I absolutely love it, I love being creative and getting grateful "thumbs up's" from my guests)

If you want to get in touch contact me any time dan@triathlon-hacks.com

If you enjoyed this book, I would be so grateful if you would take 30 seconds and leave an honest review.

Happy Training!

Printed in Great Britain
by Amazon

Triathlon for Beginners

Everything You Need to Know About Training, Nutrition, Kit, Motivation, Racing, and Much More

Dan Golding

Dan Golding is also a contributing writer at www.triathlon-hacks.com

Click here to get your **free download** on how I took 17% off my triathlon race performance by training less!

This book is for your personal enjoyment and education only. Please respect the hard work of the author.

Before embarking on any strenuous exercise program including the training described in this book everyone should consult their physician for clearance.

***

ISBN-13: 978-1484946794
ISBN-10: 1484946790